27 D STREET

A Boy, a Home, and a Village that Raised Him

By

J. ROB CASEY

27 D Street

A Boy, a Home, and a Village that Raised Him

Copyright © 2020 by J. Rob Casey

Published by Lucid Books in Houston, TX
www.LucidBooksPublishing.com

Photos of the Arnco Mill Village baseball field, the Arnco Mill Village church, and the house at 27 D St. included with permission from original photographer, Chris Loux.

ISBN-13: 978-1-953300-17-1

eISBN-13: 978-1-953300-18-8

This book is dedicated to the memory of Grandma Bledsoe, Nellie Faye Bledsoe Cole Edge (Mama), Mr. Marvin Edge and every small American town whose stories are being lost with the passage to time.

Special thanks to Susan Heffern-Shelton, for editing these stories with your amazing word wrangling abilities. And thank you to my son, Robby, for not giving up on the dream of publishing this book.

TABLE OF CONTENTS

PREFACE

Mill Villages sprang up in the early 1900s all over the United States. They were usually owned by wealthy families. The mills were built to make blankets, socks, sheets—all sorts of textiles. During wartime, they manufactured whatever Uncle Sam needed for the troops.

The villages each had a main manufacturing building called a mill, surrounded by company-owned houses where the millhands lived. There were two types of houses in the Mill Villages. One was the four-room, double-chimneyed, double back-porched variety that could house one large family or be divided to accommodate two smaller families. The other type was the *shotgun house*, so named because all the rooms were in line and if all the doors were open, you could fire a shotgun through the house and never hit anything. It had a large front room—usually the living room—a bedroom in the middle, a kitchen in the back, and a small porch behind that. Each house had a quilt or blanket closet with a half-enclosed wooden rack for stacking quilts or blankets, and shelves to store canned goods in those good old Ball dome fruit jars. When these houses were originally built, they had no indoor plumbing. Later, the four-room houses would get indoor bathrooms on the enclosed back porches.

Management lived off the Mill Village in larger, nicer homes. And at the back of each village were the houses for blacks. These houses were not offered the same upkeep as the whites' houses.

Some villages had a company store where I am sure credit was invented. No plastic cards, just a small brown paper pad with your family name penciled on the hard front page. It was easy to owe your soul to the company store. You never got out of debt. Each payday, the company would deduct what you owed so you could go charge and get back in debt again. Some villages, like ours, had small independently-owned grocery stores with gas and kerosene pumps.

There was always a church. Our village had only one. It sat at the long, sweeping curve on C Street. The Baptists went on the first and third Sundays and the Methodists went on the second and fourth Sundays. The fifth Sunday was for all-night sings, which both submerged and sprinklers attended. If you were not a submerger or sprinkler, you were just a plain sinner. If you went on the first, second, third, *and* fourth Sundays, you were either a religious fanatic like me, or wanted to make sure you covered it all just in case God saw fit to take some of each home to Glory.

There was a mill whistle—always on top of the tall black smokestack—to announce the beginning and end of each work shift. It had a distinct sound that could never be matched. All the dogs in the village would howl in unison when it went off. The afternoon whistle signaled to me that Mama would be home soon.

The water tank, positioned near the front gate, provided water for the mill and the villagers when plumbing was finally installed. When it overflowed in the summertime, all the kids in the village would go play under the overflow. It was the only waterfall we ever saw.

The hardworking mill workers took pride in their work. They didn't know they were poor until they went to the nearest town, usually the county seat.

The best ballplayers in the world played on the mill teams at our ballfield. A break here or there and old Doug would have made the major leagues. My Daddy, who I never knew, played first base on our Mill Village team. He had his nose broken several times.

Education was a must. Every parent wanted better for their children and hoped that through a high school education they might get to work somewhere other than the cotton mill. That was the dream of each parent, to get off the village to make a better life for his family. If he or she knew they would never get to leave, they worked and prayed hard that their children might someday make it off the village.

OUR FAMILY

Our name was on the list for a four-room house and after three years in a shotgun house, we all were relieved when we finally made it to our house at 27 D Street. Our village streets were in alphabetical order from "A" to "F" Street. Since we lived on D Street, I always told people that I was raised middle to upper-class.

Mama was a beautiful woman. She worked hard at the mill and looked after us as best she could. We always had clean clothes and plenty to eat, thanks to Mama.

While Mama worked, which seemed like always, our Grandma looked after me and my two older sisters, LaJuana and Mickey. Grandma weighed 300 solid pounds. She could shoot a shotgun, dress a hog, make lye soap, crochet, handmake quilts, sew dresses, use a hammer and axe, throw a knife, and cook anything she wanted. She was our dentist, pulling rotten teeth (when the Farmer's Almanac said the signs were right). She was our doctor, sewing up cuts, treating bruises and leg aches with liniment, and curing chest colds with mustard or Vick's salve plaster. She'd grease that rag and lay it across your chest—but only after she held it in front of the pot-bellied stove till it got just hot enough that it never blistered you, but always did you some good. I was always amazed at how close she could hold that rag to the stove without scorching her fingers. Her favorite medicines were things that tasted so awful you would try and get well just so you wouldn't have to take another dose. Small black calcidin tablets that tasted like a mixture of licorice and road tar; castor oil, that intestinal tract greaser and rectum exerciser. She called it a *purgative*. I called it (but not to her) *That Oil from Hell*. Her favorite and most universal medicine was kerosene. She poured it over cuts and scratches or healed a headache with a strip of paper sack soaked in kerosene and vinegar. But her all-time favorite concoction was kerosene and sugar. That was her remedy for a cough or croup. She took a large wooden spoon and put sugar in it, then poured enough kerosene on it to wet the sugar. Then, if she could catch me, which she always did—she could move it for a 300-pound woman—she would not give it to me, but hand me the spoon and make me take it myself. I always said, "Thank you, Grandma." I know she knew I didn't mean it, but she always replied, "You are welcome, son." Then she would smile and I would frown. But it did work. I thought Grandma could have been on the lead wagon of a wagon train. To me, she could do anything.

Granddaddy died when I was eight. He was a small man, only weighed about 100 pounds including his pocket watch. He was just deaf enough to get out of doing things. He wore the first pair of galoshes I ever saw. Mama said he had been a night watchman, but somehow I couldn't imagine him ever being able to protect anything from anybody.

THE KNOCK

December 24th, 1949. Mama answered the late evening knock at our mill house door. There, facing Mama with a stare that needed no explanation, was our County Sheriff. Mama dropped the crocheted potholder, turned around slowly, first to the Christmas tree, the package with his name on it, then to Grandma, holding me with my two sisters hiding beneath her shirttail. I felt Grandma take a deep breath and in a take-charge yet settling manner, asked Sheriff Potts to come in. A drunken driver had made an impact on our Christmas that would never go away.

Grandma stood out above everyone at the graveside. She knew everything there was to know about life and she understood everything about death. She knew where you go or don't go after you die. I knew she did because as I got older, I saw she had everything recorded in her large print King James family Bible. I would get her Bible down and read of all the marriages, the operations, the childhood diseases, the out-of-state visitors, and all the births as well as the deaths. I always hoped she would be around when I passed on so she could record my passing in her Bible. I figured that it was her acknowledging folks' deaths that alerted the angels in heaven so they could make room for the new arrivals. If your name wasn't in Grandma's Bible, it wasn't talked about.

Funny how older folks treat young'uns when there's been a close death. I remember when Granddaddy died. They took us to a friend's house on B Street. I remember the look on Mrs. Cook's face when me and my sisters were carried in her house. They put me to bed, never asked if I was sleepy, just told me it would be best. I remember Mrs. Cook rubbing my forehead, just rubbing it.

Somehow, I sensed she knew that only Mama kissed my forehead. About breakfast time, I heard them say that Mr. Lee had died during the night. I rolled over and faced the wooden walls, found a comforting knothole, and stared for a while. I tried to cry. I kept waiting for the surge to hit me. But it never came. I think I was too afraid. I knew deep down that I couldn't cry. At the age of eight, I was the last remaining male member of our household.

I remember hearing the word *pitiful* over and over. I was confused. All those first and third and second and fourth Sundays, where the congregation constantly talked and sang of heaven and wanting to go there. But now, when somebody does head off in that direction, all of a sudden it is *pitiful*. I'm glad it would be later in life before the word *hypocrisy* would be introduced to me. I remembered when a cousin of ours died. He had never fully recovered from WWII. He drank. He swore. He never went to church. When he died, all Grandma would say was, "Ain't it pitiful?" I felt sorry for Cousin Wayne. I knew where he was, 'cause I knew where his name wasn't.

Now that was pitiful.

A BRUSH BROOM MAKES
A CLEAN SWEEP

All Mill Village young'uns had a pet of some kind. My first pet was a small black and white mixed breed of God only knows what kind dog. Mama got him from Mrs. Sarah Yarborough's mother who lived on Temple Avenue in Newnan. After hours of in-depth thought, I finally settled on the name Ricky. Why Ricky? I don't know. But I think it was because I thought he favored one of the floppy Border Collies a little in the face. I should have known with a name like Ricky he wouldn't be long for this world.

I remember how proud I was to have my first dog. We played hard all morning long, then lay in the ditch bank and waited for my sister to walk home from the old schoolhouse near the church. One day me and Ricky were waiting for school to let out. I loved it when the old school bell rang. Ricky tried to howl like all the other dogs, but he was so young all he could do was open his mouth and let out a little squeal, like a small piglet. He did try hard though. He never lived to make a real howl.

We both saw LaJuana about the same time and Ricky jumped up to run and meet her like he always did. Neither of us saw Radford Smith and his 1940 Ford Coupe scratch-off from Mr. Harris's store and start swerving all over the dirt road, slinging rocks, and speeding down the street. Grandma saw him when he left the store and she saw him hit my puppy. Radford hit the brakes and his death-bearing coupe came to a dust-clouded halt. Stopping was his second mistake.

He got out, cigarettes rolled up in his T-shirt sleeve, cuffs rolled up on his blue jeans, white socks with the three multi-colored rings around the top, black simulated leather slip-on loafers. He had taken aluminum foil and covered pennies to make people think he had dimes in his shoes. He surely had used two bottles of Brylcreem to give his hair what he thought was a ducktail. The force of his screeching stop combined with the weight of the long hair on the top of his head now made his head like a squirrel's tail.

His smirking mouth drooped a little when he saw Grandma, or Mrs. Bledsoe as he knew her, empty the pea hulls from her apron and stand up slowly. Her brush broom was leaning against the porch rail. With a Joe DiMaggio grip, she started out across the yard toward Radford. This brush broom was village renowned. Villagers with unruly young'uns, wives with drunkard husbands, or husbands with cheating wives, could come to Mrs. Bledsoe to borrow her brush broom, with the condition they would always return it. According to Grandma, it could take the devil out of almost anything.

She stopped about five feet from Radford. I knew the exact length of that brush broom was five and a half feet. LaJuana knew that brush broom was five and a half feet. Mrs. McLendon, leaning over her porch rail, knew that brush broom was five and a half feet. Radford did not know that brush broom was five and a half feet. Radford mumbled something about *too many stray dogs in the village anyway*. The next sound I heard was the swish of a five and a half foot brush broom powered by 300 pounds of protective Grandma. It landed solidly on the left side of Radford's neck. The second lethal swing landed flush on the right side of Radford's neck. Grandma and DiMaggio were two for two.

Radford fell back against the front door of his coupe and caught himself with one foot on the running board. Grandma then pinned him against the door with her big, solid stomach. She told him to hold still and calmly asked LaJuana to go get her King

James family Bible. I was scared to death for Radford. I just knew Grandma was first going to kill him, then record his passing in her Bible. LaJuana went to the house and got the Bible off Grandma's dresser and brought it back and handed it to her. I had always heard of deathbed and foxhole salvation. Now I was going to get to see one firsthand. But instead, Grandma, still pinning Radford against the door of his coupe, handed him her Bible and a number two pencil. She made him record Ricky's passing in it. She also had him print just how it happened. After helping him spell each word, including his own name, she made him apologize to me and, with his hand on the top of her closed Bible, made him swear never to come down D Street either by foot or by car again. Radford swore. From the way he was dressed and the blood-colored places right above the top of his T-shirt neck, I suddenly realized I was looking at my first redneck.

After removing the key from Radford's car, she unpinned him and, after he got his breath, made him walk back up to Mr. Harris's store. By now a crowd had gathered out front and had watched the entire scene. She made Radford bring back as big a box as he could find. She was going to kill him for sure and bury him in the box beside the road. She told him not to leave and she went to the car shelter and got a flat-bladed shovel, even though she had a round-bladed one. He held his hands up over his face 'cause he too thought that he was a goner. Instead, she made him step over the ditch, and under my favorite chinaberry tree, she made him dig a hole six feet deep by six feet long by three feet wide.

After six hours of digging, without anything to drink, Radford had completed the job. He asked for water, and she said, "Not yet." She made him take Ricky and put him in the box. She almost made him take it back because he had brought a large Kotex box, but after remembering he could not read anyway, she made him lower the box into the hole. He spent the next two hours covering it back up. When he finished, he asked for water again. She again said, "No, not yet." He needed to do one more thing. Radford's rendition of When We All Get to Heaven was a soul-stirring experience. That in itself was pitiful.

She sent me to the house to get him a pitcher of water. The last I heard from Radford, he had founded the AMVSFTPOCA, which stood for the Arnco Mill Village Society for the Prevention of Cruelty to Animals. One of the men at the store said he would have been better off to have founded the AMVSFTPOCTRN. Which stood for the Arnco Mill Village Society for the Prevention of Cruelty to Rednecks.

BUCK

Buck was my first cousin on my mother's side. His parents were Ezra and Mildred Bledsoe, both mill workers. When Buck was born, Aunt Mildred was in labor too long and Buck ended up with severe brain damage. The first time I saw Buck, he was about twenty years old. He should have been about six feet tall, but he stood and walked in a slight stumbling crouch. It was as if he was always having trouble keeping his balance. He could not sit still. He was constantly on the move. Their yard had a gentle slope to it and if he started down it, he would fall most every time. He would fall off the porch as he tried to go down the steps. He stayed battered and bruised from his falls, but I never saw him cry. He drooled constantly. His only utterance was a high-pitched *YeeYeeYee*. He never changed expressions. He had sort of a wild-eyed stare and a half-frown, half-grin on his face all the time. I never saw him laugh. He just stared. Uncle Ezra and Aunt Mildred dressed him in a T-shirt and bib overalls. He had no control over his bladder or bowels, so they had to keep him in large diapers Aunt Mildred made from the cotton cloth scraps they got from the mill. When Buck drank or ate something, he always took paper, most times pages from the Sears and Roebuck catalog, and crumbled them up and stuck them in his food or down in his drinking glass. He never sat at the table with the rest of the family to eat.

Buck had a brother named Gerald and a sister named Margie. Gerald was cockeyed; one eye looked due east and the other due west. He was good at hiding during Kick the Cans or hide-and-seek. I reckon he could see around the corner of the house where he was hiding when the person came his way. Before games of hide-and-seek, I took two bobby pins and held one in each hand, just to the side of each of my eyes, then moved the pins away from my head ever so slowly and tried to concentrate on watching them with each eye. I was trying to get my eyes wider apart, so I could be as good as Gerald. I tried that because at school during an eye test, they would take a pencil and hold it out in front of my head and move it closer to my nose and my eyes would follow the pencil point till they almost crossed. I figured my eyes should be able to go the other way just as easy, but they never did.

Gerald and Margie seemed embarrassed by Buck if any of their friends ever came over. They never said anything, but you could tell it by the expressions on their faces and in their eyes. If Gerald got any new toys, which wasn't often, Buck managed to tear them up. He didn't really mean to. He just had no control of himself. If Gerald's new toy happened to be a small play car or truck, the rubber-tired friction-powered kind that you roll on the floor, Buck would take his teeth and rip the tires off of them. I felt sorry for Gerald, but I felt more sorry for Buck.

Uncle Ezra built a chicken wire fence around their yard so Buck could not get out. His whole world centered around his fenced-in yard at 31 F Street. Buck never left the village, except when Uncle Ezra took him riding in his old four-door '56 Buick. Uncle Ezra had taken the inside back door handle off so Buck could not open the doors while they were riding around the countryside. Me and Gerald liked to play in that old Buick. From time to time, I pretended to be Broderick Crawford of Highway Patrol and pulled Gerald or Harold Smith over for a moving violation and arrested them and threw them in the back seat, just like on Highway Patrol.

When Buck thought it was time to ride, he would start that *YeeYeeYee* sound and grab Uncle Ezra or whoever was closest to him by the arm. He didn't grab a normal grab. It was sort of a pinching grab. He was strong and could pull anybody, including

Uncle Ezra, all over the yard till he got them near that old Buick. Buck and Uncle Ezra would ride for hours, down toward Franklin and the Centralhatchee in Heard County where my family was raised. Sometimes, if Uncle Ezra did not have a lot of time to ride, he rode him to Sargent, Whitesburg, and back down the Carrollton Highway. Uncle Ezra knew a lot of people in those places because he used to drive a produce truck and those villages and towns were on his route. Most everyone he passed took the time to wave to Uncle Ezra as he drove real slow for Buck to see all he could see. If he stopped to talk to someone, they always spoke to Buck, even though they knew he could never acknowledge them or say anything back. But they always spoke.

Uncle Ezra stopped at country stores and bought Buck a Coca-Cola and a pack of salted peanuts. He tore open the cellophane peanut pack and poured them into the top of the Coca-Cola bottle. Buck had a unique way of drinking from a Coca-Cola bottle. He gripped it with a normal grip, but then he placed the neck of the bottle in the extreme right-hand corner of his mouth and just held it there, sipping and eating the peanuts ever so slowly until they were all gone. Sometimes he'd take a breath, and when he did, the gasp of air would shoot the peanuts back up toward the bottom of the turned-up bottle. It reminded me of one of those little plastic Christmas whatnots that had a Christmas scene inside and little plastic flakes that looked like washing powders, and when you shook it, it would look like it was snowing. Those peanuts moving up and then settling back down in that Coca-Cola syrup had the same kind of look. I never could drink a Coca-Cola like Buck. I envied him. Boy, could he make it last. Uncle Ezra took Buck and his Coca Cola and peanuts back home and Buck would be all right again. But only until the next day. Then, he was ready to ride.

Uncle Ezra worked the day shift at the mill from seven in the morning until three in the evening. Aunt Mildred worked from three in the evening until eleven at night. The mill supervisors and their fellow workers never complained about him leaving a few minutes early or Aunt Mildred coming in a little late; they understood they didn't need to leave Buck unattended for one minute. Every once in a while, Buck climbed over the chicken wire fence and struck out on his own. Everybody in the Mill Village knew him, and since nobody had a phone, someone always stayed near Buck, but not too close, until they could send someone to get Uncle Ezra or Aunt Mildred.

They could never go anywhere together. One went to the Sunday morning service at church, and the other went at night. They never missed a Sunday. Uncle Ezra taught Sunday School. At family reunions, they could never go together. Somebody always had to be with Buck. They were the most unselfish couple I ever knew. They sacrificed a lot to keep Buck at home. They never complained. As they got older, I could see the strain of raising Buck begin to show on them. They never wavered in their love for him and were always as proud of him as they were of Margie and Gerald.

The only person in the Mill Village that could do anything with Buck other than Uncle Ezra and Aunt Mildred was an old colored lady named Maddie Rose. She always smelled like a feed sack to me. She was a small lady who wore a rolled-up stocking on her head and a gold coin with a hole in it tied around her ankle with an old brown shoelace. She always wore an old white apron and walked with a walking stick—not a store-bought one, but one her grandson made for her out of an old poplar limb. It was about a foot taller than she was. She never used it around Buck. She didn't need to. It was as if she had Buck in a trance.

She could take him by the arm and lead him around anywhere she wanted him to go. In fact, his walking seemed to improve when she led him around. She fed him and not once did he try to put paper in his plate or glass. She sat him down in the old front porch swing and sang to him for hours at a time, always How Beautiful Heaven Must Be, Blessed Assurance, and ending up with Amazing Grace. By the last verse of Amazing Grace, Buck would be leaning on her shoulder fast asleep. She kept humming and rubbing his forehead. Buck never slept long, but he sure did seem at peace when he slept, and he looked just as normal as the rest of us. In fact, there was something manly about Buck. I sat in the cedar tree at the corner of the porch at Uncle Ezra's house and watched Maddie Rose and the angels put him to sleep. I always prayed that when he woke up, he would be normal.

No one expected it the day Buck died. It was hard to tell he was sick, as he couldn't tell anybody. Maddie Rose was swinging and singing to him in that beautiful old Negro spiritual way. As she sang the first verse of Amazing Grace, Buck lay his head on her and slowly closed his eyes. On the last verse, the one that says *when we've been here ten thousand years bright shining as the sun, we've no less days to sing God's praise then when we first begun*, a smile came across old Buck's face. It was the first time he ever smiled. It was as if God knew that Uncle Ezra and Aunt Mildred and Maddie Rose would soon be too old to care for Buck and He was calling him home to begin a better life. As I sat there in the tree watching the tears roll down Maddie Rose's cheek, I couldn't help but hope and pray that the good Lord had a Coca-Cola and a pack of peanuts waiting on Old Buck when he got to heaven.

UNCLE DOUGLAS AND THE BUG-EYED IRON LUNG

Our village was eight miles to Newnan, the county seat. We always had a good car compared to some people in the village, but we couldn't go anywhere much without Mama because she worked most of the time and always had our car with her at the mill. There was a Mr. Favors in the village that as far as I knew didn't work, except when he hired out his car to take people to town. He must have stayed busy, as he always kept a new white four-door Chevrolet Impala. He didn't have one of those lighted taxi signs on the roof of his car and he didn't have one of those mile counting meters on the dashboard, but if Mr. Favors took you to town, you knew by the way he charged that you had been taken for a ride.

Grandma's brother from Carrollton, the former mayor, ran a used car lot. His name was Douglas Cunningham; I called him Uncle Douglas. Uncle Shorty said being a politician qualified him to run a used car lot. When he got ready to get him and Aunt Myrtie a new car, he would drive from Carrollton and let Mama try out the car they had been driving. His cars always had a running board. I didn't feel so bad about our car having a running board. I told all my buddies Uncle Douglas was a politician and he got all the presidents' used cars. Everybody knew the president's car always had a running board for the Secret Service men to ride on. If Mama liked It, they would get together on price and he would drive our old car back to Carrollton and put it on his used car lot. When Uncle Douglas came just to visit Grandma, he never got out of his car. When he came to trade cars with Mama, the only time he would get out was to swap vehicles to go home in.

Uncle Douglas wore a hat most of the time. He chewed a cigar, but I never saw him light it. He just chewed it. He spoke in a growling kind of phlegmy voice. Grandma said he had a lung disorder and if he stirred around too much, he went into a heavy coughing spell and might pass out. He had this liquid bottle of stuff that the top pushed in and he would turn it upside down and spray it in his mouth if he had one of his coughing spells. Somebody told him that if he bought him one of those bug-eyed, tight-coated, loud-barking, stinking-breath Chihuahua dogs, it might help his breathing. I could never quite figure out how a dog so useless could help somebody breathe. After he bought the dog, he said it did seem to help him, so he took that little rat look-alike wherever he went. He sometimes came to see Grandma without Aunt Myrtie, but he never came without the dog.

You couldn't pet the dog except when you got in the car with Uncle Douglas. On one particular Sunday afternoon visit, while Grandma stood beside his car and talked to him, I crawled in the backseat to pet the Chihuahua. Uncle Douglas and Grandma got busy discussing whose year it was to keep the family cemetery lots clean. I eased out the back door of the car with the dog under my arm. I squatted down next to the cedar tree in our front yard and sat there rubbing the bug-eyed iron lung. Uncle Douglas finished his visit and told Grandma that he would look after the lots that year and everybody including me waved at him as he backed out of our yard. Nobody had noticed that I had the Chihuahua under my arm.

Just as Uncle Douglas's car got out of sight, Grandma spotted me holding that dog. About the same time, Uncle Douglas came flying up the hill in reverse and hit his brakes and came skidding up into the front yard. He opened the door and headed straight for me. I didn't even know Uncle Douglas could walk more than ten steps, but I was even more surprised when he broke and ran as fast as he could toward me. Just before he reached me, he bit his cigar in two. When he got to me, his face was the exact color of the faded Coca-Cola sign in front of Mr. Morris's store, sort of red with white splotches. Uncle Douglas grabbed the dog and ran back toward the car. He was sweating so heavy the color from the cloth band of his new hat was running all down the brim. He opened the car door, took off his hat, looked at the mess on the brim, and threw it as far away as he could. He might have qualified for the Olympic discus throw that year.

He was fumbling for that little inhalant bottle and the Chihuahua was yelping and barking that god-awful bark from being held so tight. The dog stuck his head down in Uncle Douglas's right shirt pocket. Uncle Douglas was so addled and breathless he forgot he kept the inhalant in his left pocket and he reached instead in the right pocket and grabbed the now quiet Chihuahua, turning him upside down, pumping his rear end, and sticking his bug-eyed head in his mouth. The dog got so nervous, he peed all over Uncle Douglas.

Grandma took control of the situation. She grabbed the delirious dog, then took the inhalant from Uncle Douglas's left shirt pocket and pumped three good sprays in his mouth. That did seem to calm Uncle Douglas down, but Grandma had to put the dog to sleep.

I got to clean up the cemetery lots for two straight years.

MUDHOLE CASH

Farther down the street from us, at the bottom of the steepest part of the hill, past the two-way stop sign that always had bullet holes in it or was always turned around, there stood the shotgun house of one of the poorest families in the village. I could never figure out how, since all the families made about the same amount of money and were provided the same things, there would be anybody poorer than us living in the Mill Village.

Grandma said people were poor for one of four reasons: liquor, cigarettes, snuff, or sex. There I was, at a very young age, already faced with one of life's major decisions. Did I want to have sex when my time came, or did I want to get rich? I wasn't quite old enough to figure out how sex could cost you anything, so I asked my friend Donald how in the world sex could cause you to be poor.

Donald proceeded to tell me about the time he walked his new girlfriend to the ballfield to watch our Mill Village team play. Along the way, he picked up $.60 worth of Coca-Cola bottles and turned them in at Mr. Morris's store. It was just enough money to buy a box of Cracker Jacks, a Moon Pie, two sticks of soft peppermint— the kind you got out of the glass jar with the shiny tin top with the red knob on top—and a Topp Cola.

Topp Cola was twice as big as a regular Coca-Cola. Mama would take a Topp Cola on trips to Carrollton or to Aunt Dura's in North Carolina so I could pee without her having to stop. My sisters never tried to learn how to pee in a Topp Cola bottle or any other type of Cola bottle, but after seeing Mrs. McClendon next door stoop to pee under her house, I discovered why. If my sisters peed like Mrs. McClendon, they couldn't have hit the

Chattahoochee River if they hung off the middle of the Carroll County Line Bridge. When I traveled in the car with Mama, Grandma, and my sisters, I got excited and had to pee a lot. My buddy's family just put in a Coca-Cola bottle for them. The Topp Cola bottle held twice as much as any drink on the market. I was too embarrassed to tell them I had a kidney problem and was nervous and had to pee a lot. I told them Mama had to use the Topp Cola bottle as the hole in the neck was bigger than the one in the Coke bottle and I needed it as my hose was too big to fit down in the Coke bottle. After seeing my buddy Luther pee one night in the ditch bank, I figured if he ever traveled with his family, they would have to take an all stainless steel Aladdin wide mouth Thermos bottle for him to pee in. I always wanted to take a trip with them just to see.

Donald went on to say that after Mr. Morris put his candy and stuff in the little brown paper sack, he and his new girlfriend started on toward the ballpark. He said his girlfriend asked him for some of what he had in the sack. He told her he was sorry, but it was just enough for him and he very seldom had any left over. He said he had no more got the words out of his mouth when she proceeded to pull him into a patch of kudzu, pulled down the front of her cutoff blue jean shorts, showed him what she had, and told him just what she would do to him if he would give her his sack of goodies. He said something came over him and before he knew it, he had given her everything he had in his sack, plus let her take a swig off his Topp Cola. He said this went on all through ball season and after the last game, Donald said he figured he had lost $8.60 and about nine pounds. He said he was thankful our Mill Village team did not make the playoffs that year. I realized then what Grandma meant about sex causing you to be poor.

I heard Grandma say she was going down the hill to visit the Cash family. She had heard Mrs. Cash was bedridden and she was going to see if she could help her bathe or help clean up the house. I asked her could I go with her and she said I could help her tote things up the steps, but I couldn't play with any of the Cash young'uns. I remember Mr. and Mrs. Cash had three girls and two boys. I guess Grandma figured the girls might try to have sex with me and that maybe the boys might try and get me to give them some of my Coca-Cola bottle money for them to buy cigarettes, liquor, or snuff. I knew that Grandma didn't want me to be any poorer than I already was.

The Cash's shotgun house at the bottom of the old red clay hill was built on high brick columns. Unlike ours, the high columns were at the front of the house and the shorter ones were at the back. I had never been to the Cash's house; I had just seen it from the road as I rode my homemade race car down the hill toward the holler. As me and Grandma walked down the hill, I couldn't help but wonder what we would find when we got there.

As we walked in their yard, I noticed that Mr. Cash had taken the body of an old 1951 Chevrolet step-side truck, cut the cab off, and buried the bed in the ground under the high front porch and made a worm bed out of it. Most everybody else that had a worm bed used old refrigerators turned over on their back with the doors taken off, but the Cashs had never bought a Frigidaire so they didn't ever have an old one to throw away.

I walked up the long front steps with no handrails behind Grandma and saw one of the Cash boys, Alvin, step from the house onto the front porch. He asked Grandma what she had in the sacks. She told him, "Hair clippers, lye soap, rags, liniment, calcidin tablets, mustard plasters, tincture of Merthiolate, Three S Tonic, rubbing alcohol, and some clothes." Alvin asked Grandma which sack had the rubbing alcohol in it and offered to carry it for her. He said he was afraid she might stumble up the steps and break the bottle. Grandma told him it was in the sack in her left hand, and I knew she wasn't telling the truth, 'cause it was in one of the sacks I was toting. Grandma never lied, but she might fib if she felt like she could get some good out of it. Grandma let him get next to her. Just as he grabbed for the sack, she took her big, hard, apron-bound belly and bumped Alvin off the top step, right into the worm bed. Alvin was so dirty and smelled so bad, the wigglers crawled out of the worm bed quicker than he did.

Grandma took her two fingers and knocked gently on the front door. After several knocks, the screenless screen door swung open, and there stood Mr. Cash. That was the first time I had ever seen him up close. Now I knew why everybody, including his own family, called him Mudhole. He wore no shoes, no shirt, and a pair of bib overalls with one gallus strap missing, causing the bib part to fall down and away from where his chest should have been. He was so skinny his chest sunk in deeper than his collarbone. He had dry snuff all around his mouth and the longest ear and nose hairs I had ever seen. He had a liquor bottle in his left hand and a rolled Prince Albert cigarette that was bent in the middle at a 45-degree angle in his right. Grandma didn't even wait for him to say come in. She just excused us and went on in. As I walked past, I looked at him and I said, "Well, since you still have your snuff, cigarettes, and liquor, you probably ain't had no sex lately, have ya?" Mr. Mudhole's face took on a more puzzled look than usual.

Somehow, even with both of her hands full, Grandma snatched me on through the door. We took the sacks on into the kitchen and tried to find a place to set them down. The chrome-legged dinette table was full, except not with food or kitchen items. Instead, there was a tackle box, the crankshaft from a '51 Chevrolet stepside truck, and the flag off their mailbox. Mr. Cash had taken the flag off the mailbox to make people think they never got any bills. Grandma noticed one of the leaves was missing from the table and asked Mr. Mudhole where it was. He told her they had taken it out and used it in the back bedroom to clean fish on.

Grandma shooed several cats and set the sacks on the floor. She took me by the hand and led me back through the other kitchen door into the bedroom where Mrs. Cash was. The minute I saw Mrs. Cash in the bed, I realized why Mr. Cash still had his snuff, cigarettes, and liquor. Her hair was the texture of the screen in our front porch door. She had snuff dripping from both sides of her mouth. The trap under her nose was full of dried snot. Hair grew out from under her left arm, but not her right. I figured her right armpit was the one she used to cup her hand and make that farting sound to entertain her and the kids, something she could do without getting out of bed. She had enough dirt under her toes to make another worm bed. Just above the calf muscle on the inside of her left leg, built with the mud off the old red clay hill, was a two-hole dirt-dobber nest. I had seen Grandma wash some filthy Mill Village young'uns, but even I wondered if she would ever get down to Mrs. Cash's skin.

I asked her if she needed me to go get more soap. She looked at me and nodded. I asked Mr. Mudhole if they had any soap in the house and he looked sort of puzzled and asked me just exactly what it looked like. Grandma told me to get a bucket of water off the back porch and take the old cast iron cooker that she saw Alvin cleaning truck parts in, rinse it out, and put it on the old potbelly stove that stood in the corner of Mrs. Cash's bedroom. Grandma took some kindling wood from one of her sacks and started the fire. Strange how Grandma always knew what folks didn't have. The mill provided all of the mill families with coal to burn, but we had to cut our own kindling. Cutting kindling was a lot of hard work, something Grandma knew Mudhole and his young'uns avoided. I went outside to the coal pile and got a bucketful, then went back in and got the old stove piping hot. The old potbelly stove began to creak and crack as the heat rose up past the two-hinged door with the spring handle, past the flat top where the cooker was sitting, and finally into the bluish stovepipe that went into the ceiling. The pipe got so red hot near the base of the stove that little specks of fire sprinkled up and down the hottest part. Grandma told me not to let Alvin or his brother Raymond know we had the stove hot because they liked to stand near the stove and spit snuff on top just so they could watch it ball up and dance across the flat top surface. I took the old coal tongs and put in another chunk of coal and got the stove even hotter. I remembered as I put the coal in how every time our load of coal was delivered to our house, I hunted through it trying to find that one diamond that might be worth enough money to get us at least a house out of the village. It was mid-August and the heat from that old stove was making it unbearable for everyone in the room, except Grandma. She'd cooked on wood stoves all her life and never broke a sweat.

Mrs. Cash's bed was close to the stove and I saw the stuff in her nose trap begin to melt. It moved like one of those glaciers I'd seen in a National Geographic book at our school library. I got near her bed to see what she was going to do with it. I was looking to see if she was as good as my buddy Luther at balancing the stuff in her trap. Luther got a trapful whenever he had a cold. He let it run almost to the top of his lip, then with a slight snap, he pulled it back just to the base of his nostrils. He told us he could do that for hours at a time and never lose any or add any to it. One time, he let us put some of Mama's cake coloring on it just to test him. It was like watching the bubble in a carpenter's level. If it ever got near the plumb line, he'd just sniff and dead center it again. Fortunately, Luther did go on to help Cotton Smith in his contracting business. Somehow after watching him balance his colored nose drippings, I never wanted cake with any colored icing on it ever again. Just plain pound cake for me.

Grandma pulled a wash pan and some rags she tore from an old sheet out of one of her sacks. She soaked the rags in the now boiling hot water on the stove. She pulled the covers off Mrs. Cash. It was clear they hadn't been changed in over a year. There, at the foot of the bed, sat three old foot-warming bricks that had been there since winter. Grandma had me stack them up under the bed, far enough that if Mrs. Cash ever did get out of bed she wouldn't stumble over them. Grandma lifted Mrs. Cash with her left hand under her neck and shoulders and gently set her up on the side of the bed.

Grandma told me to go outside and play but stay away from the Cash young'uns. I was glad to go outside because I didn't want to be in the room when she knocked the dirt dauber nest off Mrs. Cash's leg. Grandma can move fast for a big woman and I knew I wouldn't be able to outrun her.

I went on outside and sat on the top step for a while, hoping that all the Cash young'uns were gone. Grandma came to the door and told me to go home and get the kerosene can, that even her lye soap wasn't scratching the surface.

I ran up the red clay hill to our house and went to the car shelter between our house and Cousin Wayne's. The kerosene can was galvanized metal with a hexagon-shaped lid and a little tiny pour spout. It hung from a wire handle with a faded red roller to protect your hand when the can was full. Grandma used kerosene for everything. When we had the croup, she would take a big wooden spoon and fill it half full of Dixie Crystal sugar and just enough kerosene to wet the sugar real good. We had to take the whole spoonful. It would clear up a cough or case of croup right away. Grandma was always careful not to let us get too near the fireplace for several hours after we took the concoction.

I took the can from the nail and was walking back down the hill when the thought occurred to me that since this was an emergency of sorts, I should ride my wooden, rubber-wheel, rope-steering, homemade race car to the Cash's house. The race cars we made in the village used two-by-fours for the front and back axles and usually a two-by-six for the mainframe. We used any kind of rubber tires we could find. For a steering wheel, we took cloth rope and nailed it to both sides of the front axle. Our feet were brakes. The Mill Village supervisor's sons took a broom handle, stuck it in a No. 303 can, and bashed the can in around the end of the broom handle, then nailed the can to the front part of the mainframe. Then they cross-wound two pieces of cloth rope around the broom handle and tacked the ends to the upper end of the steering column. They took a wheel and nailed it to the top of the broom handle and that would be their steering wheel. It was fancy, but they never won any races down the old red clay hill.

I dragged my race car out from under the house and pulled it to the top of the red hill. I sat down and set the kerosene can between my legs, and pushed off down the hill. There was a trick to the rope steering wheel. You had to put your feet against the wooden axles and keep just enough pressure to offset the tension by pulling on the rope. It was direct positive steering and any rut, limb, rock, sand, or other road hazard could cause problems. It could pinch the inside of your ankle if you jerked back hard enough.

About halfway down the hill, at the two-way stop sign, I saw the front preacher-filled lead car of a funeral procession, followed by the pallbearers' car, the hearse, the immediate family's car, four cars of friends and well-wishers, and a flatbed truck. I could tell by the small amount of folks that whoever it was that passed away was not recorded in Grandma's Bible. They were not even coming from the direction of the church. It appeared I was on a collision course with the funeral procession of a local sinner.

Us Christians make a big deal about showing up when one of our kind is buried. Some of us show up to see how much food was taken to the dead person's house. Some show up to see what everyone else is wearing. Some show up to see if an ex-wife or ex-husband or present girlfriend or boyfriend will have the gall to show up. If the dead person had lived on A or B Street, then there was an even larger crowd, 'cause everyone wanted to hear what the remaining family members were going to do about staying in the house by themselves or if they were going to have to move. Everybody wanted a house close to Carrollton Highway.

I had gone to enough Christians' funerals and, like Radford Smith, I too could recite all four stanzas of When We All Get to Heaven. I heard the 23rd Psalm read at thirty-two funerals and I was just nine years old. I had seen preachers give altar calls at funerals, but not once had I seen anybody get saved at one of them. I thought it might be a good time to get saved, 'cause I knew God had to be looking down over the fallen saint and a new convert would cancel out the death and it would help God keep count of us. I wasn't sure how big heaven was, so it really didn't bother me when a sinner died. To me, it kept heaven from filling up so fast. I always enjoyed going to the funeral of a sinner just so I could watch the preachers squirm and struggle to find something good to say. When Cousin Wayne died, all the preacher could say after the special music was, "Here he is. Y'all come look at him."

I was hoping the funeral procession would be clear of the intersection by the time I got to the stop sign. I couldn't drag my feet to brake, because I was afraid I would drop the can of kerosene. If I dropped it and spilled any, I knew Grandma would make me pick up Coca-Cola bottles for a week to help pay for what I lost. If I dented the can, I was sure there wasn't enough Coca-Cola bottles on the Carrollton Highway between our village and Newnan to pay for a new can.

I saw Alvin Cash high up in the chinaberry tree in his front yard, eating on a new crop of berries. He hollered for his sister to go get Mrs. Bledsoe and her Bible, 'cause he was sure she was going to have to record my getting killed. That was the only good thing that might come out of this whole mess: Grandma getting to record my passing in her Bible.

Raymond Cash hollered at the top of his lungs, "Stop her, Luke! She's headed for the barn!" That was something all us Mill Village boys said at one time or another when something was about to happen quick. I saw Grandma step onto the front porch and place both hands on her hips. She then did something I'd never heard her do in my life. She hollered. Just her normal speaking voice was enough to make you mind all the time. She hollered, "Lawrence, save the kerosene! I got to bathe the rest of the family too!"

My mission's importance increased greatly at that point. I had to get down the hill, without getting killed, with a full can of kerosene. Mr. Cash got up on the top of the cab of the truck and hollered, "Ride her on down son!" Mrs. McClendon was watching the funeral procession and watching me and had to go in to take a nerve pill. When she came back onto the porch, she crossed herself. Where she learned that I never found out. I was more afraid for her than I was myself, 'cause if anybody had seen her, she would surely be kicked out of the village. Stuttering Mr. Smith, out watering his garden, tried to holler, but couldn't. The preacher riding shotgun in the lead car was waving me off. The driver of the hearse got excited and passed the pallbearers' car.

All the while, my speed was increasing. Down the hill I flew. I was approaching the intersection fast. I closed my eyes and held on. The driver of the flatbed truck never saw me as I passed under him. I nicked my head on the drive shaft, but I had not spilled any of the kerosene. I kept on flying down the hill and rolled right up in Mr. Cash's yard, just narrowly missing the half-buried painted white tires. Still at full speed, I took my right hand off the rope steering wheel and grabbed the red roller handle of the kerosene can. Grandma was standing on the third step from the bottom, her right arm out with two fingers bent ever-so-slightly. As I blew by the steps, I hung the kerosene can on her finger hooks, just like I was in an old western movie passing a mailbag to a moving train.

I gripped the rope and shoved both bare feet into the ground. There was so much mess in the yard where Alvin, his brother, and the dogs used the bathroom, my feet could not get a good enough grip to stop. I veered back onto the dirt road, holding my stinking feet away from the front axle like a wild bucking bronco rider. I had been holding on longer than eight seconds. I rolled on down to the bottom of the hill and ran my race car into the creek at the holler. I sat there for a minute, gathering my thoughts, then got off, washed my feet, and walked back up to the Cash's house. I never wanted to ride a race car down a hill ever again. When I got to the house, Alvin and his brother ran up and patted me on the back and said that was the darnedest ride they'd ever seen. I told them since they didn't have a family car, they could have my Kerosene Express race car.

I went back and sat on the porch. Grandma called me inside and handed me the bed-sheets. She told me to go outside and bury them, that she had brought new ones. It took a half can of kerosene to clean Mrs. Cash. Grandma put her on a new cotton gown, made the bed, and sat Mrs. Cash back up against the wall. They didn't have a headboard, so she put two pillows behind her back to help prop her up. She fed her a spoonful of kerosene and sugar, just for good measure.

She told me to go get all the young'uns and Mr. Cash. She made them all stand around the bed and look at Mrs. Cash and proceeded to tell them that that's how she wanted her to look every time she came back to see them. Then she took each one of them, one at a time, out on the back porch to the heavy old metal bathtub that sat on curved legs that looked like ostrich's feet. She poured the rest of the kerosene on them and bathed them with her lye soap. She cut and cleaned out from under their fingernails and toenails. She washed and shingled all their hair. She then put soda and Red Devil Lye on a rag and scrubbed all the young'uns teeth. She scrubbed all four of Mr. Cash's teeth and both his upper and lower gums. She then gave them all a new change of clothes, joyfully donated by a local Mill Village supervisor. Grandma had caught the Mill Village supervisor with the wife of the mill owner behind the church one evening and they were doing more than having a laying on of hands. Grandma even got a new apron and bonnet out of the deal.

Grandma marched the whole family back to the door of Mrs. Cash's bedroom and told them to wait outside. She went in and stood beside the bed and told Mrs. Cash to close her eyes, that there were some folks that wanted to see her and surprise her. She went back out and brought the young'uns and Mr. Cash back in and stood them around the bed where Mrs. Cash lay. She told Mrs. Cash to open her eyes. Mrs. Cash slowly opened her eyes and looked at each one of them. Then she pulled the covers up over her bosom and told them to find a seat. Mudhole and the young'uns should be back before too long.

We all cried, including Mr. Mudhole.

GEE OPAL

Every house in the Mill Village had a small spot of land. Most people used it to plant a garden. Ours was at the back of our house and ran from one end of our property line to the other. It wasn't really our property; it was the mill's, but we called it ours anyway.

The only person that had a mule near our village was a Mr. Cliff Smith. He lived behind the village, just off F Street, which was the last street. Each spring, Mr. Smith and his mule would break most everybody's garden spot for a small amount of money, plus any garden vegetables that the Mill Village folks would give him at harvest time.

Mr. Smith knew not to break a garden until he heard from Mrs. Bledsoe; she kept up with the signs and phases of the moon. He never broke a garden for anybody before he broke ours. People had to get word to Mr. Smith early because him and that old mule were in great demand, but if they sent word for him too early, he told them to wait till after Mrs. Bledsoe said it was okay or they would be wasting their time and hard-earned money.

We had a big, fine black walnut tree behind our house, just beyond the first row of the garden. When I knew Mr. Smith was coming, I climbed the tree and waited for him and Nick, his old white mule. From my lookout, I could see all the way to F Street, so I got to watch the whole trip. Nick pulled Mr. Smith on a flat wooden cart that looked like a sled with wooden runners. He carried his single blade plow and other tools on it. Old Nick's gait was so slow and lazy, I was sure glad he didn't work for Santa Claus. It seemed like it took them forever just to come two streets over. It was as if old Nick knew that the trip was the fun part and he might as well take his time and make the best of it before he started to work. That might explain why most of the millhands that walk to work didn't ever seem to be in a hurry. Nick was the only mule I had ever seen. I heard there was one at the County Fair the year that Uncle Shorty and I went, but after seeing the goats, we did not get to go where the mules were.

When Mr. Smith got to our house, he pulled old Nick down between our house and Mrs. McClendon's and stopped at our water spigot. He took a galvanized metal bucket from his sled, filled it with water, and let old Nick drink it dry. He filled the bucket four times, always standing off to the side and never getting near the back of Nick. He knew the mule would, from time to time, let out one of his long, dry, deep farts before he went to work. It sounded sort of like the mill whistle. A mule's fart is more powerful than a horse's and a lot louder than a donkey's. Even though they are a cross between the two, they have a fart sound all their own.

One day, Cousin Wayne was over at our house, drunk and planning to bareback him. I saw Nick swish his tail and fart at the same time, knocking off Cousin Wayne's hat. Just before Cousin Wayne could pick his hat off the ground, old Nick filled it full of mule apples. Cousin Wayne emptied it, all except for the one he didn't see, and put it back on his head. He went back to his front porch and sat in the swing, swatting flies the rest of the day. I laughed, shaking the black walnut tree so hard enough walnuts fell for Grandma to make a cake with no icing. During the blessing that night, I thanked old Nick and Cousin Wayne for providing dessert for us. Grandma snatched the hair off my forehead to see if I had a 666 sign somewhere.

Mr. Smith wore old, faded blue overalls, brown work boots with brass crossover eyelets, no socks, khaki long sleeve shirt with stains under the arms and around the neck, and a soiled, old, gray felt Sunday hat. When he took off his hat to wipe his brow, he revealed a two-tone bald head—tan below the brim line and white everywhere else.

After old Nick finished drinking, Mr. Smith stood around long enough to be sure the mule got rid of all his hot air, then he pulled on around back to the garden spot where he hitched up his old turn plow. He drove old Nick out to the field and surveyed it for a minute, then told old Nick to get up and they started laying off the garden. My job was to stay far enough behind them and pick up any rocks that might be uncovered. Grandma had the most rock-free garden in the world. Mr. and Mrs. Jordan's garden next to ours had new rocks in it every year. They never understood why.

After Mr. Smith broke the garden, he laid off the rows for us. This was a critical time according to Grandma, as we had to plant right away before a hard rain came and washed our rows away. Grandma had a system and a plan for everything. Grandma always led the way.

Every year before she dropped the first seeds, she walked to the middle of the garden, took off her bonnet, looked up toward where us Baptists think heaven is, and said, "Lord, please see fit to help make our garden grow so that it may provide us with vegetables for the coming year." Then she bent at the waist, took two fingers and dropped just the right amount of seeds. LaJuana's job was to take a half-handful of guano and sprinkle the amount Grandma said to around the seeds—not too much or it would burn them up. My job was to take a bucket of water and a wooden gourd dipper and water the seeds. Mickey's job was to cover up the newly planted and watered seeds with just the right amount of dirt. We had a bumper crop every year that I can remember, except the year LaJuana was sick and Cousin Wayne dropped guano for us.

Mr. Bill and Mrs. Opal Jordan, our neighbors with the rock garden, were curious people. Mr. Bill never spoke except during garden time and then it was only seven words. Mrs. Opal was a tall, thin woman with pretty dark eyes and glasses, just like Sister Rose of the world-famous Chuck Wagon Gang. I saw the picture of Sister Rose one night at a gospel sing at the City Auditorium in Newnan. I was sure it was a picture of Mrs. Jordan.

Mr. Jordan waited each year till Grandma had our garden broke so he could tell when it was planting time. Mr. Bill and Mrs. Opal had a small garden spot, about 40 feet wide and 100 feet long. Mr. Bill never let Mr. Smith and old Nick break his garden. I was glad. It was fun to watch them break their garden. I couldn't wait every year till I saw they were getting ready to turn the ground. Their neighbor, Mr. Red Yarbrough, couldn't wait either. It was a sight to see.

Mr. Bill had a small handmade turn plow and a rigged-up harness contraption made out of well rope and old belts. Just how he did it I don't know, but he got Mrs. Opal to slip the harness around her neck and shoulders. Setting the turn plow where he wanted to start, he'd hook it to Mrs. Opal's harness, twitch the homemade reins, and holler three of the seven words he said all year, "Get up, Opal!"

Mrs. Opal dug those bare toenails in the ground, leaned forward, clenched her fists, furrowed her brow, bit her bottom lip, and with all the strength in her body, she started out with a gait that would have made old Nick jealous.

I sat in the old black walnut tree for hours, watching and listening as Mr. Bill and Mrs. Opal broke ground. If Mrs. Opal got too fast, Mr. Bill hollered, "Whoa, Opal! Whoa!" If she got too far left, he yelled, "Gee, Opal. Gee!" If she wandered right too far, he hollered, "Haw, Opal! Haw!" Mr. Bill always broke a sweat before Mrs. Opal did. When the ground was broken, they would lay out the rows and it would be, "Gee! Haw! Whoa, Opal!" all over again.

They planted sort of like we did, except they used an aluminum dipper instead of a gourd dipper to water the seeds. Grandma said the aluminum was not good for the young tender seeds. They seldom made a good garden. When the plants in Mr. Bill and Mrs. Opal's garden were old enough to lay by, he hitched Mrs. Opal back up and away they went.

One year, one of the Mill Village ballplayers gave me an old catcher's mask he was about to throw away. I took the leather soles off an old pair of my work boots and used an ice pick to punch holes in the soles and tied them to the catcher's mask so they stuck out on each side. When you put on the mask, your side vision was obstructed and you could only see straight ahead. I took the mask to Mr. Bill and told him he could have it for Mrs. Opal to wear so she would not be able to eat the young tender plants. They both thanked me as he was adjusting the mask on Mrs. Opal's head.

I wondered as I walked back to my black walnut tree if Mrs. Opal could fart like old Nick.

MY BUDDY HAROLD

Most all of my boyhood playmates were, as far as I could tell, normal. To a point.

Donald had a habit of saying *forty-five* all the time. You asked him a simple question that only required a yes or no answer and he always said, "Forty-five." You could ask him to recite the Preamble to the Constitution and he would answer, "Forty-five." Ask him what his brother's last name was and instead of Doyle, he would say, "Forty-five."

I asked him one day, in the presence of Mrs. Bob Cook, who was the meanest woman I ever met, how old he thought she was. Mrs. Cook was only in her early thirties. She kept her yard swept like all the rest of the mill yards. None of us could afford those push lawn mowers with the hard rubber tires and the rotating fan blades and the T-shaped handle, except maybe the Mill Village supervisors. If you walked in Mrs. Cook's yard, she cussed you and chased you out, swinging whatever she had in her hand, whether it was a broom, mop, or butcher knife. Sometimes me and my buddies would see just how close we could get to her freshly swept yard without stepping in it. It aggravated her something furious. When I asked Donald how old he thought Mrs. Cook was, I stepped back. He gave his usual answer.

She backhanded him so hard the rivets on the back of his blue jean pockets dug four trenches twenty-two feet long across her yard, neat as a cemetery lot. Seeing those trenches made her so mad she got their wheelbarrow and made Donald haul two loads of topsoil from the holler and fill in the trenches. She then sent me to borrow Grandma's brush broom and had me and Donald sweep her yard till it was as smooth as the top of one of Mama's pound cakes. It did break old Donald from saying *forty-five*. That made him pretty near normal. It also convinced me of what Cousin Wayne said, that when he died and got to hell, he was going to find out that the devil was a woman all along.

Another not-so-normal buddy of mine was Frazier. He was born with his neck crooked to the right side. It made his right ear almost touch the top of his right shoulder blade. The first time I saw Frazier, I had a strong urge to hand him a fiddle. He looked like a natural.

One of my other friends, Ronald, was drinking at age ten. He took his Granddaddy's liquid Griffin black shoe polish, drained it through a sponge, and drank the alcohol. He drank Aqua Velva, rubbing oil, vanilla extract, and kerosene by the drum full. They just had to give him a spoonful of sugar when he had the croup or a bad cough, 'cause he already had enough kerosene in him.

Steve had an extra little finger on each hand, which may have been his secret to counting at our Kick the Cans game.

Ricky had one green eye and one almost red eye. At some point in time, he had a risen above his nose right between his eyes. A drunk doctor in a neighboring village tried to lance it and made such a mess of it that it left a big, round, yellowish looking scar. When Ricky tilted his head to the side to mock Frazier, he looked like one of those new traffic signals near the courthouse square in Newnan.

I had an almost normal left ear, but my right ear was stretched out of shape while I was being born. Mama said the doctor had to use those salad fork looking things to get me out. She said I was born almost sideways. I was so messed up none of the nurses in the nursery at Newnan Hospital would put my bassinet near the window during visiting hours. They were afraid I might scare everybody.

I did have a good friend that I really liked to play with that was not like any of us. His name was Harold. He was my Mongoloid buddy. He was the second son of Stuttering Mr. Smith. I figured if Mr. Smith was stuttering while he was having sex with Mrs. Smith, that might have something to do with Harold looking different from the rest of us. It didn't matter to me how he looked. He was my buddy. I loved him. He was happy all the time and it showed on his face.

Harold's older brother left the village before he finished high school and joined the Navy. He never came back. Cotton, another brother, was the biggest liar in the village, except when he was around my Grandma. Duren, another brother, had a slight nervous disorder from having to back up and explain all of Cotton's lies. Dale, his sister, had been raped at age six by a cousin of theirs. Someone said they thought they saw Harold's older Navy brother in the village the night the cousin disappeared. The cousin and Harold's brother were never seen in the village again.

Harold never wore a shirt. Even on cold winter days, he only wore a T-shirt. He never wore shoes. He only wore old blue jeans that were six inches too long that stayed frayed around the bottom from where he stepped on them. He had short stubby fingers on thick wide hands. He could hardly make a fist. He never brushed his teeth and they had that pond scum looking stuff on them. But it never mattered to me. I would share an RC with him and never wipe off the top. We were buddies.

When he laughed or smiled, which was most all the time, every part of his face rearranged itself. His brow wrinkled, his nose turned up, and his chin jumped out. His entire face would wrinkle up like one of those rare Chinese dogs. He would take those stubby little hands and try to cover his mouth. I loved to make him laugh.

Harold put on race car shows for me under the streetlight out in front of our house. The old streetlight had a larger, clear bulb hanging underneath a crinkled green and white cover. In the summer, that streetlight attracted all the bugs on our end of the village. All those bugs attracted the bats that hung under the roof eave at the back of our church. Harold stood under the streetlight, flat-footed on the top of his turned down blue jeans. When the bats started diving and chasing, Harold pretended he was turning a car key with his stubby little right hand. With his right foot, he pretended to press the gas pedal. Then, with his left hand, he untwisted and lowered the imaginary emergency brake handle. Again with his right hand, he pulled down the non-existent gear shift lever and put it in drive. Harold only knew how to drive automatics. With one final push of his right foot, he mashed the gas and scratched off with both feet slinging dirt and loose gravel everywhere.

When a car came up the hill, he stopped and mashed his dimmer switch with his left foot; he never mastered hitting the dimmer switch while he was running. He ran around and around the streetlight, those stout little chubby legs carrying him as fast as they could. Then all of a sudden, he came to a screeching halt and he stood there idling until another bat flew close to him, and then he'd scratch off again. He could run for hours at a time.

One night, Grandma saw his brother Cotton shoot out our streetlight with a BB gun. He tried to tell Grandma he was shooting at the bats and really didn't mean to hit the streetlight. Grandma got her three cell chrome Eveready flashlight and marched him over to the end of F Street where nobody lived. She made him climb up the creosoted pole and unscrew the burning hot lightbulb. Then she marched him back to D Street and made him climb up and put in the good bulb. She then took him to our front porch where she doctored his hands with some of her homemade butter. She took his BB gun and made him repeat one of the Ten Commandments, 'cause she knew it had been stolen. He never shot out the light again and if he ever came by and saw that it was burned out, he had one back in it before the REA could get there.

One day, Harold came by the house toting a straw basket. In the basket was one sweet potato, an ear of corn, three speckled butter beans, one butter pea, five purple hull peas, and five pods of okra. He said Cotton had set him up in the produce business. He asked Grandma if she would like to buy any of his vegetables. She looked down at his pitiful looking horn of very little, reached in her apron pocket, pulled out a quarter, and put in his dirty little outstretched hand. She knew he liked RCs and Moon Pies something fierce. He loved them, but he seldom ever got them. She didn't take any of his produce. Instead, she got me and Harold to go around back to our garden and we picked carrots, Irish potatoes, tomatoes, peppers, and a dozen ears of corn, and put them in his basket. She told him to go try and sell them and what he did not sell, take them home to his mother. "If your mom needs more," Grandma told him, "bring your basket back and I'll see you get all you need."

Harold gave Grandma that god-awful grin, held up the quarter with those pudgy fingers, and thanked her. He cranked up and sped off our porch, through our front yard, over the ditch bank, under the streetlight—just missing the guy-wire—and braked hard beside the tall globe gas pumps in front of Mr. Morris's store. He set his basket down, went inside, and in a few minutes, came back out clutching his RC & Moon Pie. He sat down on the concrete slab next to the gas pumps, eating his Moon Pie, chewing each bite like it was the last one he might ever get. He turned up that RC bottle and tried to look on the bottom to see if it had names of towns on it like Coca-Cola bottles did, even though he couldn't read. He thought they were only sold in our Mill Village.

After he finished, he tucked the Moon Pie wrapper in his hip pocket, so he could tease his brother and sister that he had eaten something they hadn't. He picked up the RC bottle, cranked up, and sped toward home. As he passed our house, he winked that wrinkled face at me and gently tossed the bottle on the row of thrift covering our ditch bank. He knew I picked up bottles and got spending money for them at Mr. Morris's.

God, I loved him.

DUEL AT ARNCO CHURCH

One of my Granddaddy's buddies and fellow Sunday school teachers was an old gentleman by the name of Mr. Houseworth. He had been in an accident at the mill and lost every finger on his right hand, except his thumb and index finger. The first time I saw Mr. Houseworth lift his hands toward heaven at church, I said to myself, "Mr. Houseworth has a natural hand pistol."

The natural hand pistol is the first toy all little Mill Village boys start out with. It cannot be bought in any store. It is a gift from Army or Cowboy Heaven. I didn't play with my plastic soldiers too much, only to play army with and when one of my buddies came over. I played Cowboys and Indians most of the time. If my buddies couldn't come over, I pretended my castrated dog Bullet was a longhorn cow. I rode my broomstick horse for hours, firing my right-hand pistol in the air, trying to get him back to the rest of the herd. Mill Village boys were born with a right- and left-hand pistol. You used the right-hand pistol most of the time because your left hand was for holding onto a store-bought broomstick horse with a red stuffed plastic head, plastic mane, and a cloth rope that hung through its mouth for a bridle.

One day, the Mill Village supervisor's son came to play Cowboys and Indians with us. He said his store-bought horse had been drug out of his yard the night before by a wild dog. I thought old Bullet would never get that play horse buried. He brought a sawed-off mop handle and stuck in between his legs to ride. Donald told him he couldn't ride the mop handle because it was a mule. It embarrassed him so bad he went home crying. The rest of ours were just plain old unpainted broomsticks, no head of any kind, no rope bridle. We just hung on to the end of the broomstick and rode. After you dismounted or your horse had been shot out from under you, you could use your left-hand pistol as well as your right. One thing to always remember was never mount up in the heat of a gun battle because you immediately lost half your firepower.

The first hand-pistol you have is a snub nose or Derringer. As you grow older, your handgun transforms into a larger gun. When your hand finally stops growing, most people end up with a .45. As my hand grew, I mistakenly took for granted that every appendage on my body would grow in direct proportion. I was wrong. I did not ride so tall in the saddle.

I couldn't wait for Sundays, 'cause I knew I would be dueling Mr. Houseworth again. I stood on the porch and waited till I could see him in the churchyard. Most of the men stood outside and talked about the past week or baseball or their garden needing rain. They talked about a fallen saint. Some of them would smoke. Mr. Houseworth never talked bad about anybody and he didn't smoke.

I started out from our house, trying to keep Mr. Houseworth's back to me at all times. Our house was in full view of the church, so if Mr. Houseworth was facing toward D Street, I had to sneak through Mr. and Mrs. Phillips' yard and come out down on C Street. If by then he had turned to talk to somebody and was facing C Street, I would go through Mrs. Gladney's yard and come up behind the old schoolhouse. How long it took me to get from my house to the church always depended on how Mr. Houseworth was talking and turning.

I climbed up the tall white church columns, where I lay in wait for him. After the church bell rang, Mr. Houseworth started up the steps headed into Sunday school. Just as he got even with the column I was hiding behind, I bellied out on the concrete slab and got ready for him to pass by. Always, just before I could pull my thumb back and take aim, Mr. Houseworth would turn, ever so slowly, hand always cocked, pointing his finger gun right at me, and say, "Gotcha!" I either got winged or fatally wounded every first and third Sunday for four consecutive years.

The day Grandma told me Mr. Houseworth died, I knew my dueling days were over. I asked Grandma if I could go with her to the funeral and she said she thought that would be nice if I would behave. She always said that even though she and I both knew I didn't have an option. When Grandma was with you, you always behaved.

McKoon funeral home had Mr. Houseworth lying in state with the casket open right in front of the altar. The church was full of fellow mill workers and village folks. I walked down the maroon carpeted aisle in a low crouch behind Grandma. I was sure Mr. Houseworth had been buried with his pistol. The closer I got to his casket, the more I thought this whole thing might be a big hoax and I would be ambushed at close range.

Grandma stood looking into the casket, studying Mr. Houseworth to see if he looked natural or not. I never understood that as nobody dead ever looked natural to me. I hid between the Masonic Lodge wreath and a large flower cross that the Finishing Department had made up out of money. The best I figured, if this was a hoax, Mr. McKoon had to go along with it and make the funeral look as real as possible.

If Mr. Houseworth's arms were placed down beside him, he might be hiding his gun in the lower half of the casket top. When he took his shot, it might ricochet and hit somebody else. I could finally get off a shot before he fired his second round. This was my chance! When Grandma turned to walk away and speak to the family, I made a quick leap forward, knocking over the Masonic

Lodge flower arrangement and hanging by my arms on the side of the casket. I slung my right leg up and over and straddled the side of the casket, getting ready to fire. But I never got off a shot.

Sure enough, Mr. Houseworth's right arm had been placed by his side, pistol ever ready, but unfired. The Masons had placed their mystery cloth on his stomach, his left arm draped on top. In his left hand, he gripped a new Bible with three fingers, leaving his index finger and thumb cocked and aimed right at me.

He never moved, but I swear I heard him say, "Gotcha!"

AMEN CORNER

Mamas in the Mill Village never considered formula or bottles for their newborns. They knew breastfeeding was the oldest and best way to feed and nourish a baby. A visiting preacher came to our church to hold a revival one year, along with his wife and their new baby. She led the singing and sat right in the front of the church in the choir director's pew below the choir loft. When her baby got hungry, which babies seem to do a lot, she breastfed him right there in the pew.

We were really young, but even me and Donald noticed an increase in attendance in the Amen Corner while the visiting preacher was holding the revival that year. The Amen Corner didn't fill up because of his preaching either. The Amen Corner was the first few pews on the left side. To look at the preacher, you had to stare right toward the choir director's pew.

I thought you had to be able to say a real resounding *amen* or your *amen* had to be different from the others before you could sit in the Amen Corner. Some of the *amens* were more like *amahn* or *aaamen*. My favorite was the double *amen* Mr. Jackson gave from time to time. He said it like it was spelled with a "d" on the end. You knew the preacher had really said something worth listening to if Brother Jackson hollered out in that deep bass voice of his, "Amend and amend."

I asked Grandma if they had tryouts for the Amen Corner and if they had amen practice, sort of like choir practice. She just looked at me and did one of those long, heavy-breathed sighs, like she did when the questions I asked were not worthy of an answer.

Nobody in the Amen Corner hollered this particular revival. They just sat there, spellbound, like they were in a trance or something. The only time they looked like they were paying attention was when the preacher's wife fed her young'un. After the revival that year, attendance really fell off.

One night, during church conference, a discussion came up, I believe under new business, about how attendance had been falling off. I thought church conference was a bad time to talk about anything especially church attendance, because if the conference had been announced the Sunday before, like it was supposed to be, most times there wouldn't be enough members to show up for a majority vote on whatever was brought up. Baptists are a peculiar people. I think that's in the Bible somewhere. If they want something in particular, they will fuss and fume and cause a stink in the church and have their little group at the conference so they can all vote just alike. But if a conference does not include anything of interest to them, they won't even bother to show up.

My Mama was the church appointed clerk, writing down the minutes of the meeting. I never figured out why they called it the *minutes*. It should have been called the *hours* because that's how long those conferences lasted. There was nothing more boring to me and my buddies than to have to sit there and listen to the minutes of that last conference being read and then adopted. I noticed that the same people in their own little groups always made what was called *the move*, and the same people always made what was called *the seconds* on whatever they wanted to get passed. You didn't realize it so much while it was happening, but at the next conference, there it was in black and white.

Something needed to be done about church attendance and nobody could come up with anything. After I saw that this subject was going to end up like most subjects at a conference—tabled for discussion—I got my buddy Scooter to stand up and suggest that, based on the way the Amen Corner filled up during our last revival, every woman in the church who had a small baby should sit in the choir and breastfeed. We would have to enlarge our parking lot, set up folding chairs, and add on a balcony.

Scooter's mother fainted, his father, without thinking, nervously lit up a cigarette, and Mr. Jackson hollered, "Amend and amend!"

GRANDMA MOSES

Me and Grandma could hardly believe what we saw as we watched the heat lightning over Arnco church that night. Instead of lightning flashing down from the sky or streaking across the sky like veins in a leaf, we saw lightning flash straight up from the front of the church. The flash of light did not disappear, but instead stayed fixed, lighting up the big white column where I used to hide to ambush Mr. Houseworth. Before I could ask Grandma what she thought it was, she said for me to stay put and up from the swing she stood, straightening her apron and grabbing her brush broom as she went. I remember seeing her silhouetted against the old church, lightning flashing, brush broom in hand— her staff. She walked with authority like God himself had summoned her to go see what was taking place at His house. I thought, *that's probably how old Moses looked when he headed off into the wilderness, staff in hand, sure of where he was going, but not sure what he was going to find when he got there.*

Hmph. Grandma Moses. Not a bad ring to it.

The way I figured it, I had two options: either stay on the porch and be of no help to God or Grandma, like either of them needed it, or take the Zacchaeus route. I knew I had to get a closer look, so I headed for the chinaberry tree behind Mr. Morris's store.

The tree was surrounded by white picnic tables in the churchyard. They weren't fake redwood tables, but genuine all-day-eating, fifty-foot long, hand-hewn churchyard tables. The kind big enough to set two number two washtubs side-by-side at the end, one full of honest-to-goodness, hand-squeezed lemonade, and the other filled with tea so thick with sugar you could drink it or take it home and pour it over your pancakes the next morning. Some of the men of the church would go to the Newnan icehouse to get blocks of ice in thick brown paper bags for each washtub. The bags had a wet smell all their own. I knew whatever was going on at the church, it was not an ice delivery. It was Friday night, and even though we were having an all-day sing Sunday, I knew the ice wouldn't last that long. Not even in those brown paper bags.

From my perch in the lowest fork of the chinaberry tree, I could make out Grandma approaching the dust-shrouded light at the front of the church. I knew right away by the way she was gripping her brush broom and walking around she wasn't seeing no burning bush.

The church sat at the end of a big sweeping curve on C Street. It was tough to make the curb at any noticeable speed, day or night, even when you were sober. Mr. Pritchett had just proved that you couldn't make it at all if you were drunk. Especially at night. Mr. Pritchett had been over on the Carrollton highway to buy groceries from Mr. Whittle's store and had stopped at Mr. Morgan's beer joint to buy enough beer to last him the weekend. Apparently, he had tried to drink most of his three-day supply before he left Mr. Morgan's. From the looks of him, I was surprised he made it over the wooden trestle bridge that led from the Carrollton Highway into the village.

Most bridges had a name, and even though it was smaller than most, this one had a name too. We had named the old creosoted bridge, the Marvin Dingler/Harley Davidson Memorial Bridge. Marvin Dingler got drunk one night and tried to jump his Harley over the bridge onto the Carrollton Highway. He got a running start at the stop sign at the top of the hill where a road with no name crossed with C Street. He sped shirtless, shoeless, and helmetless down the hard dirt-packed road. The only thing he had on was a pair of blue jeans and a pair of underwater goggles he had borrowed from one of the Mill Village supervisor's sons. Not the divided two-eyed kind, but the full-face smelly, blue rubber kind with the plastic lens that would fog up on you if you happened to try and breathe through your nose. At full speed, about halfway down the hill, Marvin's goggles fogged up so bad he didn't see the load of sand the county had piled there to fill in the ditch bank. When he hit the sand, the Harley laid on its side and continued over the bridge without Marvin. Marvin skidded about halfway up the bridge on his chest, arms extended and legs bent up like a skydiver I saw at an Armed Forces Day Parade near the National Guard Armory in Newnan one year. He came to a stop just before the peak of the bridge. He didn't even get to see his Harley as it crossed the Carrollton Highway without him.

He got Mr. Favors to take him to Dr. Hammond's in Newnan to get all the creosoted splinters picked out of him. Dr. Hammond, who was real educated and book-learned, knew about all the new happenings in the world. He knew Robert Ripley was just starting a Believe It or Not! museum in St. Augustine, Florida, so he wrote a letter and sent all the splinters to Mr. Ripley. Mr. Ripley wrote back and thanked him, but just wanted to make sure all those splinters really did come out of just one person. Marvin left town for a while, but when he returned, he would tease all the Mill Village girls by showing them his chest and telling them he had been in a fight with a tiger at the Grant Park Zoo. Cotton Smith backed him up on it.

I knew we wouldn't rename the bridge for Mr. Pritchett, even though it had to be a trick for him just to drive over it, but I was sure that at the next church conference, someone would bring up a vote to rename the church. Mr. Pritchett had run his 1957 two-tone Ford right up the front steps of the church, the grill of it resting squarely in the double doors. As far as I could recall, that was as close as he had ever come to going in.

He climbed out of his car and stumbled down the steps, holding on to the side of the car like it had handrails. He tried to close the trunk, but couldn't. He rubbed his eyes and started around the passenger's side of the car where he stumbled over the jack that had been thrown out along with all his groceries. Still on his hands and knees, he reached for a crushed can of tobacco. Grandma planted her right foot across his knuckles before he could lift it off the ground. All 300 pounds of her had Mr. Pritchett and Prince Albert both pinned on Holy Ground.

Mr. Pritchett slowly looked up, first at the black leather three-quarter height shoe (that can only be bought at Forman's department store in Newnan) then at that hard, solid workbench of a stomach that kept all the wrinkles pressed out of her apron, up past the bound bosom that was the lifeline to seven children, then to the solid, square jaws that never twitched in fear or anger. It didn't matter if Grandma had her teeth in or not, those jaws stayed square all the time. Even drunk, Mr. Pritchett recognized flared nostrils when he saw them. Quickly passing them, he stared into the brightest blue eyes in the world, eyes that could coldly pierce right through you or be warm, caring, and understanding—whatever the situation called for. I knew by the way he was shaking and holding his chest what kind of eyes he was seeing. I shivered a little myself.

He blinked. She didn't.

Still on his hands and knees, he looked slowly from side to side. He saw other people had gathered out on the side of the road by this time, but no one ventured near him or Grandma. It was as if they had been spiritually stopped from coming any closer. They seemed to know they were approaching hallowed ground. Mr. Pritchett looked a little uncomfortable from being stared at and a lot uncomfortable from having 300 pounds of a Godsend standing on his hand. He gently knelt his right knee to the ground and again looked up at Grandma. He blinked twice this time. Grandma didn't. She had not blinked since she got up out of that swing.

I eased down the chinaberry tree and hid under the picnic table. I knew something was about to happen. I didn't know exactly what, but with the weather like it was and the eerie feeling I had, I didn't want to be sitting in that tree in case God did send forth a bolt of lightning to liven things up a bit. Mr. Pritchett, kneeling and staring at Grandma, tried to say something, but when he opened his mouth, nothing came out. It was as if God knew that if he did try to explain what happened, it would be a lie and God had seen Grandma's brush broom in action before and I think even He knew Mr. Pritchett was going to catch enough wrath as it was.

Grandma slowly lifted her foot off Mr. Pritchett's hand. He looked at her, still with his mouth open, but not talking. She nodded for him that it was all right for him to try and stand. He peeled his hand off the ground. The underside of it looked shriveled and wrinkled, like when you stay in the water too long. Grandma stepped back as Mr. Pritchett slowly began to wobble up. With both hands, she stretched out her brush broom, sort of like old Moses would have done with his staff to turn it into a serpent. I think Mr. Pritchett had heard enough radio preachers over WCOH preaching about Moses because he tried to cover his eyes with his good hand.

Nobody knew it, but Burvin Hyatt had gone into the basement of the church and was trying to get up the stairs to ring the church bell so as to alert the men in the village. The church was the place where everybody met whenever there was an emergency. The lights in the '57 Ford had been burning for a while now and the rebuilt Western Auto battery was quickly draining. As Grandma stepped toward Mr. Pritchett with her outstretched brush broom, the lights in the car went out. Burvin rang the church bell, and a lightning bolt hit the chinaberry tree I had been sitting in.

I wet myself, rededicated my life, and prayed hard for Mr. Pritchett's soul, all at the same time. I just knew that God and Grandma had turned Mr. Pritchett into a pillar of salt, or caused sores to come up on him, or something else really biblical had happened to him.

I was wishing I had my pad and a pencil to record firsthand what I was going to see when we got enough car lights in the churchyard so I could send it to Mr. Ripley, 'cause I knew even he wouldn't believe this. Instead, when enough cars had pulled into the yard, all I saw was Mr. Pritchett, sweeping up his trash with Grandma's brush broom. She was helping him decide what was still groceries or what was now trash. I crawled over and picked up a can of sardines and stuck it in my shorts' pocket and eased on back to the house. I couldn't see how God would punish me for stealing from somebody who just tried to knock his house of worship down. As I walked back to the house, I wished Cotton had been there to see God silence Mr. Pritchett when he was about to tell Grandma a lie.

Mr. Pritchett and his family were in church on Sunday. But this time, he left his car outside.

A MOVING EXPERIENCE

One of my favorite pre-fantasy era pastimes was to sit in the front porch swing and watch the cloud formations over our Mill Village church. Every kind of cloud in the world formed directly over Arnco Church. Some evenings, I lay in the swing on the front porch and when the clouds passed over, I picked out old ladies' faces, elephants, dogs, horses, and depending on the direction of the wind and the type of cloud, the face of the Old Master himself. Me and Grandma had seen Him one evening in a thunderhead.

Grandma told me to look back up toward Newnan where the sky was a charcoal gray and look directly over the old oak tree at the edge of the churchyard. She saw Him before I did and just stared for a while. She took her right arm and pulled me up to her side and hugged me real tight before she showed Him to me. I saw Him right away and I tried to get even closer to Grandma. I was afraid He might be headed to get me and I wasn't sure I was ready to go. I told Grandma to tell Him, if He would, to please take somebody else in the Mill Village beside me. Maybe Cotton. Or Mrs. Cook or somebody. Then I told her I didn't know if I was ready to go and started crying real loud. She stooped down, bent from the waist, legs straight, like she always did, and told me to stop squalling like that. What we were seeing was just a cloud. She said if I looked around, I could see the Old Master in a lot of things, not just clouds.

I remembered thinking I had seen Him in the cedar tree one night while we were playing Kick the Cans, but it was just Donald with his sister's wig on. It still scared me though. Grandma said for me not to worry yet. If I was ready to go or not, when the time came for me to know it, I would. She told me to just keep going to church with her and Mama and my sisters and something would happen somewhere sometime to let me know it was time for what us Baptists called *getting saved*.

We all went to church the next Sunday and after I got out of Sunday school, I went down the hall into the basement to the men's restroom. The basement had a musty smell all the time. You could smell it over the pine disinfectant. The urinals in the bathroom had rusty iron-laden water stains in them. I asked Grandma if the toilets in the ladies' basement bathrooms had rusty stains in them. She told me they did not. I figured it had something to do with our glands. Grandma never used the word *testicles* and she wouldn't let me say *balls* around my sisters, so I had to call them what she did, *glands*.

I went on upstairs and waited for the church bell to ring. Our church had a steeple with the finest sounding bell in the world. The bell only rang on Sundays and village emergencies. I hoped one day to be able to ring the bell. I felt it would go a long way toward getting me into heaven. If I had failed miserably in life and Gabriel lost his ability to blow his trumpet, then God might let me into heaven just on bell ringing alone.

After Burvin Hyatt rang the bell, I found Mama and Grandma near the front of the church on their row. It's funny how church people get mad if someone gets their pew or someone gets their parking place in the churchyard. It didn't matter if a visitor did it, they still got mad. I remembered going to the First Baptist Church in Newnan one year for an R.A. meeting and none of us from the Mill Village Church thought we could sit anywhere. Every pew had a little gold plate with someone's name on it, either donated by or in memory of. Our R.A. director sent me outside to see if he had parked in somebody's marked parking place. We stood in the back of the church, even though there were seventeen empty pews.

Scooter told our members at the next church conference that they made us stand up at the First Baptist Church. It made some of the good brethren so mad they voted for us to pull out of the Church Association. They dang near voted to call Nashville, the Baptist Vatican, and secede from the Southern Baptist convention all together.

I took my place on the fifth row on the right side and sat between Grandma and Mama. After the Sunday School report, morning prayer, and special music, the preacher asked if anyone felt like they wanted to testify. Baptists, on occasion, have what they call *a testimony time*. The preacher asks for volunteers to stand up and tell the church what the good Lord has laid on their heart. I figured that preachers, like anybody else, from time to time got tired of their job and needed a break, so they did one of two things: have a sing or testimony time. That way it wasn't necessary for them to study and pray and ask the Lord to help them prepare the message. I got to ciphering that if every preacher in Coweta County asked God to help them prepare a message every time they got in the pulpit, including funerals (but not weddings, as they always said the same thing, just changed the names) and every time God had to give them something different to say, then there wouldn't be enough time for God to do the other things He needed to do. So a sing or testimony time gave God a break too.

We had a fine old gentleman in the church that repeated himself when he testified. He was not a genuine stutterer like Donnie Bussler, he just, just, just said words over and over again. The preacher avoided Brother Smith. If several members stood up at the same time, but if the Spirit had not followed the members through those two inside swinging doors, Mr. Smith, who was always good for twenty to twenty-five minutes of testimony, would be recognized. I asked Grandma why the church had swinging doors on the inside and she said it helped ease the drunkards when they came in on special occasions, like Easter, Christmas, funerals, or weddings. On this Sunday, testimony time was going good and Mr. Smith had not been recognized yet. Every time he stood up with somebody, the preacher called on the other person, even if Mr. Smith stood up first.

A fine old saint of a lady in her eighties, Mrs. Strickland, stood up behind me. I saw her out of the corner of my eye when she started waving her hands about shoulder height, slowly to the left, then shifting slowly to the right. She stood directly behind me. She began to lightly clap her hands, shifting and clapping, clapping and shifting. I was beginning to get in the spirit myself. This might be the time Grandma had talked to me about. Mama sensed something I had not and she placed her right arm around me. Just as Mrs. Strickland was clapping and swaying to the left, I was looking at Mama's arm on my shoulder, waiting for Mrs. Strickland to rebound back right.

That's when it happened.

About halfway through her sway, I felt the hairs on the back of my neck trying to swap pores with each other. Goosebumps the size of carbuncles started alternating jumps up and down my arm, sort of like the lights on the sign at the beer joint where Cousin Wayne used to go. Then a warm sensation, heavier than sweat, engulfed my glands and a larger wet spot appeared on the front of my britches. All that was followed by a sudden urge to reach for anything that resembled toilet paper. We didn't have printed church programs like I had seen at the First Baptist Church, but we did have McKoon Funeral fans stuck in the songbook racks. I grabbed one with one hand and stuck two fingers in the communion cup holders, trying to steady myself and gather my senses.

Mrs. Strickland had shouted and I had shit myself.

The firmer Mama mashed my shoulder trying to hold me still, the more determined my colon was to finish pushing out what was left of three pancakes, one glass of milk, a banana, a popsicle, two mayonnaise sandwiches, one Nehi grape drink, one pound of seedless grapes, one box of Cracker Jacks, one bowl of turnip greens, three pieces of cornbread, and three Zero candy bars that I had eaten the day before. The shoving match between Mama and my colon lasted for over five minutes. My colon won.

I couldn't speak because Mama placed her left hand over my mouth when God alerted her that Mrs. Strickland was about to unleash a world-class shout. I knew I was in the Lord's house, sitting between two saints and surrounded by a lot of other saints, but I couldn't help wondering, *What the hell was that?* I never heard a shout before. Tears were flowing all around me because of the surge of Spirit that had just passed through the swinging doors, and into and out of Mrs. Strickland. Mama, misty-eyed, misread the strained look on my face and saw the tears coming from my eyes. She leaned over and asked, as only a mother can, "Lawrence, tell me what you're thinking." I shook my head slowly from side to side and again she asked, "Please, son. Tell me what you're thinking."

By this time, some sort of order had been restored. Mrs. Strickland sat down and the good sisters and good brothers three pews forward and four pews back were now listening to a mother ask her small son how he felt and just what was he thinking after such a religious experience. Again, I shook my head in a Mama-don't-make-me-talk kind of motion. Pinching my shoulder as only a mother can pinch, she said in an almost irritated voice, "Now tell me, son. Talk to me." I looked at Grandma for a sign and she nodded approvingly for me to mind my raising and to always tell the truth, no matter how much it hurt. She knew Mama wanted me to show out a little amongst her church friends. Grandma said, "Go ahead, Lawrence. Tell your mother what you felt and what you were thinking after Mrs. Strickland shouted."

I tried to swallow real hard. I looked around at all the folks looking at me. Then I said, "Yes'm." Mama and Grandma sat back with pride. I smiled and took in a long, deep breath like some of the men smoking in the churchyard did. I said, "Well, first I shit myself and then I asked myself, 'What the hell was that?'"

After Grandma revived Mama by sticking some Vicks Salve up her nose, and after they sent my sisters home for a changing of underwear and a clean pair of husky blue jeans, they took me to the altar and gang-prayed over me for two straight hours, with Mr. Smith praying the last half hour.

We only went to the Methodist services for the next five Sundays.

GRANDMA AND VISITING PREACHERS

Us Baptists go by Robert's Rules of Order, the Baptist bylaws, and the church covenant. I never could understand the meaning of any of them, but I knew one thing for sure: they didn't have any room for a woman being a deacon. If they had, Grandma would have been the pope of all deacons. She knew the Bible backwards and forwards. She knew who killed who, who married who, and who begat who. I couldn't figure out what *begat* meant, but it sounded interesting. The only Bible version to Grandma was the King James version, the way she could recite it, I thought he might have helped her write it. She had an answer for everything and could back it up Biblically. She knew if the preacher's sermon came out of the Bible or if it came out of Nashville. I couldn't wait for a visiting preacher to come to our church, because I knew Grandma would know more than he did and would set him straight if he got out of The Word.

I often wondered why the deacons voted to let visiting preachers come to our church. I thought if they weren't good enough to have a church of their own, then why on earth would they let them come to ours. I'd just as soon hear a Gideon speak. At least then, I got to see how many different colors and sizes they were still printing Bibles in. I always managed to look real pitiful in front of the Gideons so they would feel sorry for me and give me a brand new New Testament.

Cousin Wayne sent off for an application to join the Gideons after he bought his beer joint. He said he had more church members as customers than anybody else, and buying the beer joint did make him a businessman. He said most of his church customers were from Sargent, our Mill Village neighbor toward Carrollton.

I rode my big-tired Western Flyer bicycle over to Sargent one day and saw one of our deacons at a local beer joint. I spoke to him, but he let on like he didn't see me. The next Sunday, while we were waiting for church to start, I saw him outside, talking with the preacher and some of the other men at the church. He saw me coming and turned completely around and tried not to look at me. He turned his back every time I tried to get in front of him. I walked around him more times than I had at the cakewalk at last year's Arnco/Sargent Halloween Carnival. I decided to put a basketball move on him like one Alvin and Alton Bishop did to each other in their backyard. You just move left, stop real quick, then quickly jump back right. He took the fake, and there I was, standing right in front of him and the preacher. I said good morning to the preacher and looked at the deacon and told him the next time he needed a bottle of liquor, I was sure Cousin Wayne's beer joint would be closer than having to drive all the way to Sargent. He just laughed and rubbed the top of my head, which I hated, and followed me up toward the church. He was about to backhand me until he saw Grandma out of the corner of his eye. She heard the whole conversation and told him that if he laid a hand on me, his liquor buying days would be over before Burvin could ring the church bell. I could tell he wanted to try her, but I think he remembered last Saturday when a two-truck traveling Gypsy circus had come by our Mill Village and set up near the holler. Grandma won the arm wrestling contest, the hatchet throw, the shooting contest, and the nail hammering contest. He was mad and couldn't do anything about it, which made him even madder.

Not one to let a good situation pass, I followed Grandma up the steps of the church and turned around and pooched out my lower lip at the deacon, fever blister, and all. Grandma saw me. She yanked my huskies down and shook my shirttail. (That was what she called a whipping.) I stood up the entire service while she fanned my rear end with a funeral home fan. I saw Cousin Wayne the next Tuesday and he thanked me for his new customer and gave me a quarter.

The next Sunday, we had a visiting preacher that preached on every bad woman in the Bible, from Lot's wife to Delilah to Bathsheba, and finished up with my favorite, Jezebel. Early on in life, Grandma told me never to go with a girl with any of those names. The visiting preacher spoke down to all the women in the church and belittled them and told them about how sorry they were if they acted like any of the women he was talking about. He said that every great man since the beginning of time had taken a fall because of a woman. I was loving it because I couldn't wait to see what Grandma was going to do. All during the service, the women fidgeted nervously in their pews. All except Grandma. Some got up and pretended to go to the bathroom, but not Grandma. One lady even left the church altogether, the preacher pointing his finger at her as she slunk out the back door. I don't believe Grandma flinched, blinked, or even breathed the whole service.

He finally quit and asked the piano player and song leader to come up and lead the congregation in a verse of Just As I Am— the song most people rededicate their lives or get saved to. Before the first chord was struck on the old upright, Grandma was out of her pew and headed down front. Everybody knew she was the most saved person in the church and never needed to rededicate her life. They knew, just like I did, she was fixing to make a Christian out of that visiting preacher.

He didn't know Grandma. I watched him stick out his right hand to shake hers like was customary. Grandma was about a foot taller than the man, so she leaned down over his shoulder to whisper in his ear. I couldn't tell what she was saying, but I saw the preacher's face turn from white to red, back to white, then to red again, which is where it stayed. The veins in his neck and the side of his head filled up and stuck out like the veins on Mr. Cliff Smith's mule's leg. The preacher got up on his tiptoes and then eased back down again. Grandma was gripping the preacher's shaking hand so tight that sweat began to pop through his double-knit suit. He tried to pull back, but she pulled him forward and gripped him a little tighter. He acted like he was trying to get down on one knee to pray for her, and about the time his knee almost touched the floor, she tightened her grip and up he came on his tiptoes again, waving his free arm over his head. Grandma pulled him up close to her, then let go of his now smaller-than-normal right hand, bear-hugged him, picked him up off the floor, then acted like she was Pentecostal and fell slain in the Spirit to the floor, still holding on to the visiting preacher. All 300 pounds of her fell right on top of him. It was a move I had seen Freddie Blassie put on Dick the Bruiser in a newsreel between Westerns at the Alamo Theater one Saturday. Except Grandma took the preacher down faster and harder.

I jumped over a pew and ran up to the front of the church and squatted down near Grandma's head. She opened up her right eye and gave me a twinkled wink. I pretended to pat her cheek like I was trying to wake her up. She moaned slightly, rolled up, and sat straight up in the middle of the preacher's stomach. His legs recoiled and he bent forward from the waist. Grandma stumbled up and pretended to be a little woozy. She stepped back on his chest to get her balance. As the deacons revived the preacher and helped him up, she turned back to him and said, "Powerful prayer, preacher. Powerful prayer."

The chairman of deacons had to dismiss the service and then shake everybody's hand at the front door. The visiting preacher was propped up against the deacon in a half-crouch, like a leaner horseshoe. He wasn't wanting to shake anybody's hand. On the way out, all the ladies took his right hand anyway and gave it a good shake. I heard the visiting preacher ask the deacon who they would be having Sunday dinner with. He turned pale and almost fainted when the deacon told him they would be eating at Mrs. Bledsoe's. He knew her now.

Me and my sister ran on to the house; Grandma and Mama had already beat us there. They had prepared their usual Sunday feast: chicken, fried steak, a roast, candied yams in thick sugar syrup, collards, butter beans, corn fixed with a lot of butter in that old iron skillet, baked apples with the core out, rice pudding, biscuits, and cornbread. She made fried peach pies, the kind you folded and mashed together with a fork, then stuck the fork in the dough to let them cook through and through. She made a coconut cake and a pound cake with fresh strawberries for topping.

We all sat down with the visiting preacher and chairman of the deacons as our Sunday guests. Grandma asked me to say the blessing, and I said, "God is great, God is good, Let us thank Him for our food. By His hands we all are fed, thank you God for our daily bread. And God, please bless the preacher's shaking hand." Mama kicked me under the table. It didn't matter if I was at one end and Mama was at the other with ten people between us, she could always find my leg and kick it.

The preacher had trouble eating left-handed so Grandma cut his meat for him. Every time she started for his plate with a knife, he closed his eyes. He didn't eat too much meat for dinner. When it came time for dessert, he asked for one of those fried peach pies. Grandma knew how much I loved them, so she told him she was afraid they were too brown on the bottom and offered him a piece of pound cake instead. He told her that would be fine and she cut him a generous piece and dipped out a big spoonful of strawberries for him.

She had been to West End Supermarket in Newnan with Mama and bought the first can of pressurized whipped cream we'd ever seen. We always poured cream or milk on our strawberries and pound cake when we had it before. The preacher fumbled to get the red plastic cone-shaped top off the can. He tried not to grip it too tight because his hand was still numb. He pointed the can at his saucer and nothing happened. Grandma took the can from him. Instead of putting her fingers on top of the nozzle and pushing down, she put two fingers under the bottom of the nozzle, pointed it toward his saucer, and pulled up. The whipped cream flew right over the pound cake and strawberries and hit the preacher right square in the chest. It stuck dead center in the middle of his horse head tie. I hollered and Mama kicked me again.

Grandma got up, went to her knife drawer, and walked back over to the preacher with the biggest butcher knife she had. I could see her Bible on the dresser through her bedroom door and figured I would be the closest one to it if she needed it. The preacher froze as her hand started toward his neck. Starting at the knot, she took that knife and scraped ever so slowly downward. About halfway down his tie, right above the whipped cream, she stopped, looked him in the eye, and said, "Preacher, this morning, I got your message. Now, do you get mine?" He moved his lips in a *yes ma'am* shape, but not a sound came out.

After dinner, she hand-washed his tie for him and helped him soak his hand in Epsom salts. She packed him a take-home sack, including the whipped cream can.

Boy, that Grandma could preach when she had to.

KICK THE CANS

There wasn't a lot to entertain you in the Mill Village. We didn't have a lot of store-bought toys, and we didn't get to go to town much, so sometimes we had to invent things to keep us busy. Most times it kept us out of trouble, but sometimes, the things we invented were the very things that got us in trouble.

We played ball, made race cars from two-by-fours and old wheelbarrow tires, and played chase. We even built a pretend Olympic site on some of Mr. Border's property out on Welcome Road. We dug us a pit and filled it with pine straw for the high jump and pole vault area. Steve used a big bamboo cane pole to help clear him over the homemade stick bar. We made us some hurdles, and we used a big rock the county had dug up while they were grading the road for our shot put. We were the only country represented, so we got all the medals. We used Coca-Cola bottle caps for the gold medal, 7-Up caps for the silver medal, and Dr. Pepper caps for the bronze.

When we were running short of medals, we stood around Uncle Shorty's store and waited for someone to start to get a drink from the old Coca-Cola box. We talked about how good and cold the last bottle of whatever cap we needed was, how it had ice in it and everything. The next thing you know, they changed their mind and bought what we were talking about. We took the cap holder off the side of the cooler and fished out the cap we needed. It helped cut down on expenses.

On Sunday nights after church, a lot of the families gathered up next door to the Kings' house to watch the Ed Sullivan Show. The Kings had the only television on D Street. While the grown-ups were watching television, we played chase or a game of Knock the Can, using oil cans and a broomstick. If we didn't have a broomstick we called it Kick the Cans. If you never wanted to be the It person, you came to play with shoes or a stick. One of the Mill Village supervisor's sons would always show up with a stick and shoes.

To play Knock the Cans, you began by stacking up four green and white Quaker State thirty weight high detergent 100 percent aluminum oil cans. Those were the days before 10W-40 and paper oil cans with aluminum ends. The cans' popularity dwindled with the invention of paper cans, and when plastic oil containers with the neck spout came out, Kick the Cans was quietly laid to rest.

The Mill Village supervisor's son always wanted to be It. It made him feel big and important. Nobody else ever wanted to be It, but we never let on. So my buddy Steve invented a counting system for choosing the It person. He counted the number of us that wanted to play, then pointed his index finger at someone and chanted, "My mother told me to pick YOU," which was exactly seven words. It didn't matter how many of us there were, Steve's final count always ended up on the Mill Village supervisor's son. He had it down to a science. One night I had four cousins over from Carroll County, plus our six regular players, which made a total of ten. I was nervous for Steve, 'cause we never had more than seven players before. What's more, of the ten, four had no shoes but had sticks, four had shoes but no sticks, and the Mill Village supervisor's son was there, all shod and armed, not with a broomstick, but with a steel axle from his race car. Luther had no stick but had a left shoe and only a right sock. He lost a big toenail from being It and shoeless the Sunday night before when the Mill Village supervisor's son had to go home sick with diarrhea after eating the chocolate candy squares we had wrapped up for him. Steve told Luther he could not be counted but could still play. That left all ten of us to play, but only nine counted. I stood there beside

Steve, three players to our left, three players to our right, and Luther and the supervisor's son across from us. I counted to myself and knew if Steve started from the left, he would miss the supervisor's son by three people. If he started from the right, he would miss him by two. Steve winked at me and asked me to trade places with Luther. He said by Luther standing next to him, he would be sure not to count him. Then he started slowly to his right, skipping over Luther, slowly pointing his finger and chanting. I thought, *Call Mr. Ripley, 'cause Steve's finally going to miss one.* But, instead of going in order, Steve zig-zagged around to all eight of us, ending up square on the supervisor's son. It was the slickest piece of counting I had ever seen.

Steve went on to work for the local bank. When he retired after only six years, moved to the Bahamas, and bought a big house, the supervisor's son—who was by then a supervisor himself—was the only one of our Kick the Cans gang that seemed surprised.

After the It person was chosen, someone would kick or knock the stacked up cans over and everyone would run and hide while the It person gathered the cans and stacked them up again. The blows from the broomstick and hard, leather-bottom boots dented the cans and made them harder to stack. The longer it took to stack the cans, the longer you got to look for a hiding place. If the It person found you or chased you down and touched you, then you had to go to jail, which was our front porch step. You only got out of jail if someone got past the It person guarding the stacked up cans and knocked or kicked them down. The game ended when everyone was caught or the cans were dented up so bad you couldn't stack them anymore. Even then we got some use out of those old cans by stomping in the middle of them with our boots on to make us a pair of aluminum shoes.

My favorite place to hide was under our house. I never got caught because the It person didn't know about my secret hiding place. I would have been only a marginal Knock the Cans player if our house had not been built on brick columns. I was a slow runner, but I could usually make it to the rear of our house where the tall brick columns supported it. Then I would crawl under the house and go all the way up past the shorter columns to my spot behind the front porch steps. From there, I could tell who was in jail and watch how far the It person wandered away from the stack.

There was the stump of an old tree that had been left there for some reason. It stuck out of the ground and looked petrified. It was the shape of the clay mountains of Arizona that I'd seen in some old John Wayne movies. I always wondered why it was the only one left under our house. Over the years, I dug out around it and played with my army men, using the stump as my lookout post.

One night, as I lay on my stomach peeking out between the crack in the steps, I heard someone crawling toward me from the back of the house. I wondered who had found my secret hiding place. I heard a solid thud that can only be made by hitting your forehead on a beam. From the squealing sound the person made, I knew it had to be a female. If a boy had hit his head, he would have practiced cussing for a while. After a few whimpers and sniffs, the shadowy figure began moving closer to me. I whispered for them to tell me who they were and a tearful voice said, "It's me, Imogene." It was my sister's friend from E Street. I told her to keep quiet, but to come on up where I was laying. Imogene was a pretty girl, poor like the rest of us, but she had a certain look about her that made her different from any of my sister's other girlfriends. Even at ten years old, I was beginning to notice girls were more fun to look at than boys. It hadn't hit me yet as to why, but every so often a funny feeling would hit me, sort of like the feeling you get from smelling bedding fish for the first time. You know you're supposed to do something, but you don't know where to start or what to do.

Imogene slid up beside me and I rolled over on my back and slid sideways to make room for her. I slid right. She slid right too. I slid again. She did too. The next time, I slid up next to my tree stump and came to a stop. She slid over next to me again. I figured she was just scared or something and still hurting from hitting her head and just wanted to be close to someone. I lay there on my back and pulled one of my plastic army men from under me—the one kneeling, holding the bazooka on his shoulder. I sat him on top of the stump. I told Imogene not to say a word 'cause the supervisor's son might hear us through the cracks in the stairs. We lay still for a minute. I felt Imogene move over on her side and turn toward me. She took another one of my plastic army men— the one laying on his belly with his legs spread out, shooting a rifle. She pretended he was crawling up my leg. The army man started his patrol around my ankle, and I was okay. He crawled up over my shin to my knee, and I was still okay. But when he began to crawl over my thigh and down the inside of my leg, all of a sudden that fish bed smelling sensation came over me again. I knew it was dark under the house and I thought maybe Imogene was having trouble seeing where she was playing with that plastic army man, so I moved her hand and the sharpshooter back on top of my leg. Without hesitation, she pretended the sharpshooter had slid back down the hill. He was now crawling ever so slowly up the perfect trench of my two shaking legs. She stopped the sharpshooter about an inch from the bottom of my zipper and took her two fingers and walked them up over and around the zipper of my husky blue jean. She whispered that it was a scout looking for action. As any soldier that has been in battle will tell you, it was hot. A cold sweat broke out on my forehead.

I felt her take my zipper tab and whisper, "What's this? An opening to an enemy cave?" She proceeded to start pulling down the zipper. About halfway down, a certain part of me stood halfway up. She began to breathe heavy into my ear and for some reason, I breathed even heavier. She took my Talon zipper on down, then reached through and under the front of my Fruit of the Looms. She took what she called *the enemy soldier* in her hand and gripped him like she was trying to choke his head off. She whispered that she had captured the enemy and now she had to punish him. She held onto me with her right hand. With her left, she undid her belt, unbuttoned her shorts, and slipped them and her panties off in one motion. I could tell right away this was not her first war maneuver. She whispered that she had to make the soldier suffer. She gripped him harder and pulled on him, slow at first, then harder and faster. She asked me if the soldier had been punished enough. I tried to remember some of the Geneva Convention I heard my POW Uncle Shorty talk about. I gave her only my name, rank, and a made-up serial number. It must have made her mad because she went to work harder and faster, and with each stroke, the thought of smelling bedding fish got more vivid and clear. I closed my eyes and dreamed I was in a boat on the Chattahoochee River, hunting bream beds. The smell of the fish bed seemed to get stronger and stronger. I felt as if I was right on top of the fish bed.

Slowly, I opened my eyes, and through the dim light coming in through the cracks, I could see that Imogene had positioned herself directly over me and my enemy soldier. She leaned down and told me that now she was going to put my soldier away for a while. I wasn't sure what she meant by being *put away*. With my soldier still in her hand, she started to straddle me. With her still hanging on, I rolled to the right, firing my first and last shot. I missed her but hit my own bazooka soldier on top of the stump. She let go of my now spent and slumping soldier and pulled up her shorts. As she crawled out from under the house, she mumbled something about *looking her up when I learned how to play army*. I thought I had really done something by keeping my soldier from being put away.

When the game was over, I told all my buddies about what Imogene tried to do to me under the house. When I got to my hiding place during the next week's game, five of my buddies were laying flat on their backs, holding a plastic army man in their hands.

SPENDING
THE NIGHT

The closest I ever came to having sex again was when I went spending the night. Spending the night was when one of your buddies would ask his mama if he could ask your mama to let you come over and spend the night with him. Usually it was on a Friday night, never on a school night, and seldom on a Saturday night, unless the folks you were spending the night with were going to church the next morning. It didn't matter if they were submergers or sprinklers, just as long as they were going to church. You never got to spend the night with a buddy if his daddy was a drunkard. Mama and Grandma would always come up with a good-sounding reason for you not to go to your buddy's house if his daddy had a drinking problem. They would never say anything to hurt his feelings. Usually they made up some reason for you to ask him to come to your house instead. It never did make sense to me since the time spent together would be the same regardless of whose house you were at.

One evening, Barney, my good friend from A Street, came over and asked Grandma if I could spend the night with him. Mama was working the evening shift, so Grandma made all the decisions after three in the evening. Grandma knew Barney's folks and she knew they both played the guitar and sang at church and that Barney's older brother had joined the Air Force and that they always drove a good clean car and she never heard anything but good about the whole family. Besides, Barney was my business partner.

When I was ten and he was twelve, we would walk all over the village and pick up Coca-Cola bottles and take them to Mr. Morris's store where he would pay us three cents apiece for them. We would work the ditches every day from A Street to F Street. We never were allowed to go to the colored part of the village. We were told that colored folks did not drink Coca-Colas. Never why they didn't, just that they didn't. I was eighteen years old and in the service before I ever saw a colored person drink a Coca-Cola. I rushed to the phone to call Mr. Ripley. He called me racist and hung up on me.

Grandma said it would be all right for me to go spending the night with Barney. It was four streets over from our house to A Street and me and Barney picked up six dollars worth of Coca-Cola bottles before we got back to his house. If I knew then what I know now, I would have gotten lifetime right of way contracts on all the ditches in the state and could have been a millionaire by now since recycling has become so popular. But I thought back then that when Knock the Cans went out with the invention of those plastic containers, there could never be a future in aluminum.

Barney's house was built on a high bluff overlooking a valley where the railroad tracks ran. After supper, we stood on the hill and saw who could pee the farthest toward the tracks. If you could pee to the closest edge of the crossties, you were okay. If you could pee to the nearest rail, you were good. If you could pee to the rail farthest away, you were pretty good. If you could pee to the other side of the crosstie across both rails, you are extra good. Barney could always pee to the rail farthest away. I could pee over the ditch bank on the other side of the track. I took the head of my hose and pinched it on both sides, and with all the pressure I could muster in my lower stomach, I shot a flat stream over the ditch, regardless of the direction of the wind.

When Coca-Cola bottle business got slow in the wintertime, we held pee contests. Barney rounded up some of our Mill Village buddies and bet them he could out-pee me. Mill Village young'uns would bet on anything. He stopped by my house and got me, telling the other kids that he needed a fair and impartial judge. He knew that living with Mrs. Bledsoe made me real honest. When we got back to Barney's house, he and the other kids stayed at the top of the hill and I crawled down the bank and far enough out of the way to judge the contest. After they decided what they were going to bet, Barney let the other kid go first to see how far he could pee. Then he peed, pretending to strain real hard, but letting the other boy win. I crawled back up the hill and me and Barney fussed, him acting all mad, pretending to try and convince me that he had won. I looked back over the hill and Barney bragged on how good a pisser the other boy was, how he never saw anybody pee so far before. The other boy really started to gloat. Mill Village life did not allow you to have many proud moments, so you seized every opportunity you could.

Barney suggested that maybe I give it a shot. I said something like how my Mama made me squat to pee 'cause I didn't have enough force to keep from peeing on the front of the toilet seat. That got the other kid real brave and he bet everything he had in his pocket he could out-pee me. We had a way of working them for everything they had. They got so sure of themselves that some of them went and asked their parents to let them have some change and got their piggy banks full of pennies. When Barney thought there was enough money for the both of us to split, he took the wages and told the other kids to go pee. My pinching method never failed. I cleared the far side ditch bank every time. One kid said he was going to send my name to Mr. Ripley.

One night after supper and after I out-peed him again, Barney said he wanted me to show him how to pee that far. I told him just to take his hose and pinch it on both sides until the hole was about two-thirds closed, then just push and pee. I noticed Barney got real close to me just to look at what kind of grip I used.

Before bed, we went out on the back porch and passed the longest, loudest gas I ever heard a person make, almost as long and loud as Mr. Cliff Smith's mule. Me and Barney covered our heads with pillows to keep his daddy from hearing us laugh. There were three long, deep blasts followed by a short, crisp, snappy one. The dog howled. Barney's mother came running to see if we were all right. She said she thought the train derailed. She said that was always a horror of hers. Barney's daddy came and told us to go to bed and walked on to their bedroom just like nothing had ever happened.

Barney's bedroom was in the back of the house. The train passing by at night always woke me up, but it never seemed to bother Barney. I guess he was used to it. We lay down and Barney's mama came and kissed us both good night. Me and Barney laughed ourselves to sleep.

I hadn't been asleep long when I woke up with a funny feeling in my stomach. The sensation I had when Imogene tried to crawl on top of me was fast approaching. I could hear my heart thumping. I could feel my hose standing up, just like it had done every morning of my life as far back as I could remember. But this time, something was different. It wasn't moving up and down by itself. I blinked to make sure I wasn't dreaming. I did a quick hand check and realized both my arms were folded behind my neck. I turned slowly to my buddy and realized that he was having a nightmare of some kind. He was moaning and groaning and yanking me up and down. He breathed heavy and flared his nostrils. Through the dim moonlight, I saw him grit his teeth, smile, and frown, all at the same time. I realized he had his hands down the wrong set of underwear.

Remembering my manners, and knowing how people get upset when you wake them from a deep sleep, I decided it wouldn't be right to wake him up. I was just going to let my old buddy sleep. Just keep on sleeping and dreaming. The problem was, I finished the dream before Barney did. I lay there wondering just how far over the railroad track that would have flown. I just knew from the force of it that I would have cleared the tracks, the ditch bank, the pine thicket on the other side of the tracks, and probably hit the top of Cousin Wayne's beer joint over on the Carrollton Highway.

I figured that would have caused Barney to wake up, but he just kept moaning and groaning and pushing and pulling. Finally, the feeling came back to my lower body, including my hose and glands, and there I was, enjoying Barney's dream with him again. Just about the time I learned to flare my nostrils, and moan and groan, and grit my teeth without chipping them, and just about the time I was going to let her fly again, Barney sighed one big sigh, shuddered, and finished his dream. His hand stopped cold, but I lay there, still fully primed. I peeled Barney's fingers from around me, eased the covers back, and crawled out of bed. I gently opened the back door and ran to the hillside to try and hit the beer joint again. About the time I was ready, Barney's mama stuck her head out the door and shined her six D-cell ultra-high beam Eveready flashlight on me standing there in a half-crouch, jockey shorts around my ankles, hose in my hand, nostrils fully flared. Somehow I didn't think she believed me when I told her I just slipped outside 'cause I was afraid I might pee on her toilet seat.

Breakfast sitting across from Barney's mother the next morning lasted two light-years.

SLOP JARS AND
SLOP BUCKETS

When Mill Village houses were first built, there was no indoor plumbing. Each shotgun house had its own two-hole outhouse. The four-room houses, set up for two families if needed, had two one-hole outhouses on opposite sides of the back lot. If only one family lived in the house, most times there wasn't a problem getting in the outhouse. Except around the time when Grandma gave everybody a round of castor oil. I think the reason it was called "a round of castor oil" was because if you needed to go real bad and somebody was in the outhouse, you had to circle around it at a very fast pace until it was your turn. If you were sick, you got a round. If you weren't sick, you got a round to keep you from getting sick. It didn't make sense to me. If you were the one that wasn't sick, the castor oil ended up making you sicker than the one that was sick. I don't think Grandma gave us so much castor oil until she heard that a doctor's job was called "a practice." It seems to me that's what she was doing to us, just practicing.

I hated to go to the mailbox and find the new Sears and Roebuck had just been delivered. That's when we got our biggest round. I tried to remember each year about when to expect Mr. Buggs, our mailman, to stuff that 400-page prescription in our box. If I saw it delivered, I took it out and buried it under our house. Cousin Wayne's family next door got two catalogs. I really felt sorry for them.

There is nothing harder to do than to try and clean yourself with a slick page of a Sears and Roebuck catalog. If you used too much pressure, the whole page would slide right up your behind, or slip out of your hand, which caused a mess in itself. I always took a few corn shucks in with me just to finish the job. Funny how different family members used different sections of the catalog. Mama used any page except the one with the ladies underwear. Granddaddy used only the tool section. He was afraid Grandma might see something she needed fixed and the right tool for the job would end up in his hands. He hated work. My sisters used the tire section unless they were mad at me, then they would use a page or two out of the toy section. Those were my favorite pages to look at while I was sitting. I always used the sheet or towel section. It seemed to make the catalog pages feel a lot softer. Grandma always used the yellow index pages. They did not have the slick finish on them and they really were the softest. Everybody respected her and left them for her.

The two-hole outhouse seems like a good idea, but it was a waste of time and lumber. Using the outhouse was a one-man job. I've been to as many all-day singings as anybody. I've been to day and night revivals. I went spending the night in houses with as many as fourteen people in them. Not once have I ever seen both holes of a two-hole outhouse occupied at the same time. Patience, mind games, and muscle control skills were refined waiting outside an outhouse door.

The outhouses were usually built two garlic bulb squeezings from the main mill house, where the cold Northeast wind blew directly toward the mill house, and the southerly winds blew away. While a great deal of time was spent in an outhouse, there never seemed to be a great deal of effort put into building one. They were never painted, except at the Mill Village supervisor's house. The wood used was two grades lower than barn lumber. Most times, they had a two-hinged door with a threadbare wooden spool and nail for a pull handle. Sometimes they had a cutout in the door that looked like a half-moon. Ours had one. One day Grandma tightened the top hinge on the door and it straightened the door to where it would swing shut by itself. The cutout didn't look like a half-moon anymore. It looked like a capital C, which I'm sure stood for castor oil.

There were no windows in our outhouse. You froze in the winter and suffocated in the heat of summer. The only time I looked forward to going to the outhouse was in the spring of the year. Grandma took some sweet shrub blossoms, tied them up in a handkerchief, then squeezed them real hard and hung them in the outhouse. They gave off a sweet smell that deodorized the place. When the sweet shrubs were all used up, she did the same thing with gardenia petals. They seemed to last longer.

Going to the outhouse was easy enough in the daytime, but at night it could be quite a trip. Even though I knew it was the same distance, the trip always seemed twice as long. I was sure I heard noises like the ones at the Grant Park Zoo and imagined all sorts of creatures waiting to get me. When I had to use the outhouse at night, I alerted everybody in the house that I was dying with the leg ache. All my husky blue jeans had oil stains from all the liniment that Grandma and Mama kept rubbed on my legs at night. I cried and carried on about how I believed I couldn't walk to the outhouse without somebody helping me. Grandma got up and walked with me to the back door and stood there watching me until I got back. I usually had to explain how I could run so fast with my legs aching like they were.

One night, as she watched me go to the outhouse, a pack of wild dogs ran between me and the house, headed toward our chicken pen. Grandma went back inside and got her shotgun, then eased down the steps to stop the pack of dogs from getting her setting hens. My sister heard the dogs barking and got up and found the back screen unlatched. Not knowing me and Grandma were outside, she latched the screen and went on back to bed.

As Grandma fired into the pack of dogs, I made my break. I was glad my legs were greased with liniment as I was sure I would have blistered them running as fast as I was. I got to the top of our back porch steps and tried desperately to open the screen door. Between the yelping of the buckshot-filled dogs, the shooting of the shotgun, and Grandma hollering, "Get from here, sir!" I wanted to get inside our house worse than I ever had. I took my hands and pulled at the bottom of the screen door and wedged my big toe in the crack. I could see Grandma running back toward the house. She ran out of shotgun shells, but grabbed her hoe handle and was swinging away at that pack of dogs.

A stray out of the pack came running to the foot of the steps. He looked as afraid as I was, but I knew he wasn't. I let go of the door and my big toe got wedged between the screen and the door facing. I couldn't move. I prayed hard that God would let me be James Gaddy just for one minute. He lost his big toe in a lawnmower accident. Knowing I was in real danger trapped by the wild dog, I did the only thing I could: I fainted.

Cousin Wayne, awakened from his drunken sleep, looked out his bedroom window to see Grandma swinging her hoe handle and me laying there slumped on the top step. He turned around to Cousin Coreen and said, "I knew Cousin Artie would break Lawrence from crying with the leg ache one day." He was about to send word to McKoon Funeral Home when he saw me move.

After I recovered, Grandma said the next time she got to go to town, she would go by Johnson Hardware and buy us something so we wouldn't have to go outside at night to use the outhouse. I asked if I could go with her so we could go by and tell Mr. McKoon we almost had to use him.

The next Saturday, we got Mr. Favors to take us to town in his taxi. He let us out in front of the hardware store and Grandma told him to be back in thirty minutes; that was all the time she needed.

We went inside and she headed straight to the back of the store and began to look at funny-shaped metal pans. They didn't look like the cooking pots she and Mama used. I asked her what they were and she said that the smaller pot was called a chamber. The other one was taller and was painted a slick-looking white. It had a white lid with a red trim around the edge and a little finger grip handle made into the top. It looked like there might be enough between the handle and the lid to pry open a Coca-Cola bottle. You could save the caps in the pot. It looked right away more useful than the chamber. I asked Grandma what it was called and she said it was a pot, but most village folks called it a slop jar.

I knew what a slop bucket was, we had one. It was a five-gallon metal bucket, usually a large can, with a wire handle with an unpainted roller. We put table scraps in our slop bucket. It hung on a big nail right outside our back door. I don't care how much of what kind of scraps you put in the slop bucket, it always smelled the same—a real strong, sour smell that reminded me of dressing a hog right before you cooked it. Mr. Cliff Smith came by the village houses every few days and picked up everybody's slop to feed to his hogs. Then he had Beavers Packing Company in Newnan slaughter and wrap his hogs and take it back to the village to sell the meat. Grandma always talked him down a few cents because she reminded him it was her good slop that helped get his hogs so fat. She knew how to save a dollar. It helped Mama on the grocery bill.

Grandma bought the slop jar and as we walked back out to Greenville Street, I didn't feel quite so poor now. The mill owners had recently taken the shutters off our house and put in new glass windows that raised up and down. And now we finally had a pot to pee in. Mr. Favors took us on back home and as we rode over that old wooden Hill Bridge, I felt a little safer knowing that when night fell, I wouldn't have to fear going to the outhouse anymore. I told

Mr. Favors I couldn't wait till dark. He looked at me real strange and drove on off.

I carried the pot up high for Mrs. McClendon to see. I thought if she peed inside as much as I did outside I bet her pot had to be rusted out and seeing ours might make her want a new one. Cousin Wayne saw me and called me over to his house and asked if that was a new ice bucket. Anything that Cousin Wayne could put ice in and hide his beer from Cousin Coreen was an ice bucket to him. Vases, stovepipes, cast iron pipes the county would leave by the road—anything that would hold ice and beer—he would find a way to stop up one end of it. I told him what it was and what it was used for. I knew from all the beer that Cousin Wayne drank that he needed to use a slop bucket instead of a slop jar.

I took it to the back of the house and asked Grandma where to put it. Would we hang it on the nail out back beside the slop bucket? That seemed to me like the place it needed to be. She said no, we would put it under the bed during the day and at night we would put it on some old Newnan Times-Herald papers on the screened-in back porch.

I played hard the rest of the day. It was hot, so I took a Coca-Cola cap and tapped it onto the water spigot. You had to take the cork out from under the Coca-Cola cap to get the best spray. If you turned the water on too fast, it would force the cap off. Grandma showed me just how many times to turn the tap. Then everywhere the top was crinkled, water squirted out and I had me a shower to play under. I drank a lot of water and played real hard. I drank more than usual because peeing at night was no longer a problem for me. At supper, I drank lots of iced tea and Mama even commented on how good a supper I was eating.

After supper, I got the wash pan and bathed and put on some new underwear and hopped in the bed. It wasn't even dark yet. My sisters told Grandma that I was in the bed and it wasn't even dark yet. Grandma came through the door and before I could tell her I was just waiting to be the first to try out our new pot, she shoved two big wooden spoons of castor oil down me, turned the back of her hand and felt my forehead, rubbed my legs with liniment, and checked me all over for ticks. She just knew I had to be sick. I closed my eyes and she kissed me and went on back into the kitchen. Mama came in with my snickering sisters and kissed me, and told me she hoped I got to feeling better and for me not to forget my prayers. I never opened my eyes. I hated to see my sisters enjoying themselves.

Way on into the night, the castor oil woke me up. I could tell I didn't have to do a Number One, as they made us say in school when we had to go pee. I knew right away I had to do a Number Two, as Mrs. Jones, my first-grade teacher had taught us to say when we had to do a sit-down job. I thought whoever invented that call of nature numbering system got the thing turned around. The Number One is always for the most important. When you played ball, you were the best if you were chosen Number One. If your team came out on top, you were Number One. In a foot race or horse race or even a race to be in the front of the lunchroom line, if you got there first, you were Number One. The President's office is the Number One office in the land, while the vice president is Number Two. In order of urgency, degree of difficulty to hold, places to do it, and the fact that you needed a paper or something to finish the job, I felt like a Number Two should have been a Number One and a Number One could even have been as low as a Number Three or Four. It just made better sense.

As I lay there with my stomach rumbling, I kept thinking the urge to pee might hit me first, but the constant pressure of fermented castor oil looking for a place to go overshadowed any thoughts about peeing. Careful not to spread my legs too far apart, I slid both legs over the side of the bed and eased onto the floor. I shuffled toward the back porch like a bound-footed Japanese geisha girl. As I made my way back, I realized me and Grandma had not discussed if a Number-Two-Now-Turned-Number-One was permitted in our new slop jar. As I got nearer to it, I didn't see anything to make me think I could. No catalog. No extra Newnan Times. No corn shucks. I cussed it as I went on by it. Wild dogs or not, I had to GO.

I made it to the top of the steps and did not think I heard a dog bark close by. I was dying. I reached for the slop bucket on the top nail and balanced it on the top step. Grabbing the handrail, I crawled up on top of the slop bucket and did my version of a Number One. But I didn't pee. I was determined to be the first to use our new pot. I hung the slop bucket back up on the nail and went back into the house, knowing I would never eat any of Mr. Smith's pork again. I got some of the Times-Herald off the floor from around the pot, cleaned myself, then opened the screen door and threw the paper out back, hoping the wind would take it away during the night.

I turned around, still holding my water, and went back to the pot. I gently lifted the lid and set it on the floor. I centered myself above the pot and started to pee. As my water hit the bottom of the pot, a sound like I had never heard played up the sides and out the top. It was a high-pitched singing kind of sound, like a musical note. The bottom of the pot was slightly raised in the middle. The closer you peed to the center, the higher pitch the sound, and the farther away you got from the center, the lower the note. I played nine verses of Barbara Allen before I ran out of water keys.

The next morning I saw Cousin Wayne sitting on his back steps, reading a section of the Newnan Times-Herald. He was holding it by just the tips of his fingers, as far away from his face as he could get it.

THE DENIM
PASSOVER

Grandma had every potted plant known to man. She lined them up on the porch in those red clay pots with the hole in the bottom. I didn't know the names of any of the flowers or ferns, but I did find out what an elephant ear plant was. I was helping Grandma water the plants one day, using a Maxwell House coffee can. We didn't have a hosepipe. Mill Village people called water hoses *hosepipes*. I'm not sure where the term came from, but if you looked real hard at a hosepipe, whether it was rolled up or stretched out, the name just fit. I was watering the elephant ear plants and for some unknown reason, I leaned forward and took a big bite out of a big hard green leaf. My mouth caught fire instantly. I would have given anything to have a hosepipe douse the flames in my mouth.

Mrs. McClendon had a hosepipe, but she had to keep it hidden because every time her grandson Ronald came over from Banning Mill, he hooked it up and stuck the nozzle down the front of his pants and turned it on wide open. He stood there grinning as the force from the water flushed around his glands. Grandma said pretty soon after Ronald got married, his wife left him because when he washed the dishes in their new fancy house near Whitesburg, he took the dish rinsing hosepipe and stuck it down his britches.

Grandma saw I was on fire, so she sloshed the half-full Maxwell House coffee can in my mouth, then sent my sister Mickey in the house for the butter dish. With two fingers, Grandma dabbed a half-pound of butter on my lips and gums. She used those two fingers for everything. With a swipe of those fingers, she could clean out a chicken, front and rear, or clean the homemade cake batter from the top of her mixing bowl. She used them to shoot a toss during a game of Carrom. They were used as a measuring cup, vice grips, and now they were being used as a fire extinguisher.

All that butter on my lips and gums set my talking back two months. I was just beginning to talk a lot, but the butter greased my mouth, lips, gums, teeth, and tongue so much that I couldn't get a grip anywhere to make a word come out. Grandma thought something in that elephant ear plant affected my brain. About the time I got the butter drooled off, Grandma double-fingered me another round. Once she got me cooled off, she reminded me not to do that again. Like I needed reminding.

Between Mama and Grandma, most everything that needed doing around the house could and would get done. They could lay linoleum rugs, fix plumbing, put in new pull chains on the lights that hung on brown cloth-covered wires from the ceilings, and hang a swing. They could do anything.

One Summer, our front porch needed reflooring. It would be a big job just to find a place to put all of those pots during the job. Grandma told me that I needed to help. I couldn't wait to move the elephant ear plant. When Cousin Wayne saw us moving the plants, he came over to help. Cousin Wayne was so drunk, Grandma got him to agree to help pay half of the costs. I think Cousin Wayne did it because he knew Grandma would write about us getting a new porch in her Bible. She would write what year it was put in and who all helped fix it. Cousin Wayne just wanted his name to be in her Bible somewhere.

With Mama working double shifts and Grandma canning so much, they decided to hire a jackleg carpenter who was an old retired millhand in the village. Even though our front porch was on ground level, Mr. Warren showed up with a ten-step wooden ladder tied to the roof of his old DeSoto. He wouldn't need it, but just having it around might make you feel like you were getting your money's worth. He looked the part, in his felt hat and nail apron from Hudson Hardware full of assorted nails, and blue Sears and Roebuck overalls—the ones with the pencil holder on the bib and the folding rule holder on one leg and the claw hammer loop on the other. He kept the cuffs rolled up to catch the sawdust. You can tell a painter from a carpenter by the color of their overalls. Carpenters' overalls were always blue. Cotton Smith wore a blue denim coat over white overalls. He was the first general contractor I ever saw.

The day Mr. Warren started the job was hot and muggy. When Mama came home between shifts to get her lunch sack, I heard Mr. Warren ask her if she minded bringing him a glass of water. He sure was thirsty, he said. Mama was a beautiful woman. Everybody in the Mill Village knew that after my daddy was killed, she spent all her time working and trying to raise three young'uns. It bothered some of the people in the Mill Village that Mama did not date. It never seemed to bother Mama, as I heard her say over and over when people asked her about it. When she got us all raised, then she might have time to find just the right man.

I was sitting in my favorite chinaberry tree, the one that Donald Jordan knocked me out of while playing Kick the Cans one night. I had to hide there as all my buddies had taken over my hiding spot under the house. Donald was the It person and got mad because he couldn't catch anybody. He picked up one of the Quaker State oil cans and hurled it into the chinaberry tree, not knowing I was up there. The hard rim of the oil can hit me above the right eye, knocking me out cold. I fell from the tree like a shot squirrel.

I saw Mr. Warren hand Mama the empty Bama jelly drinking glass, the one with the green and red flowers on it. As she turned to go back to the kitchen, I saw him follow behind her. All of a sudden, I heard a scream. Mama yelled, "No! Stop!" I sailed out of the tree, jumped over the sawhorse, and ran into the front room, afraid of what I might find. Mr. Warren had Mama cornered against the wall, trying to kiss her. I could tell by the look on Mama's face that she had never considered having a carpenter for her second husband. She was trying to push him back, begging him to leave her alone.

I ran around the other side of the house and into the kitchen where Grandma was still checking the seals on her jar lids. They always sealed. I told her what I thought I was seeing. She wiped her hands, put down the dishrag, and took off her apron. The only time Grandma took her apron off was when she was going to bed or when she was going to kill and dress a hog. She didn't want bloodstains on her linen apron. When she took that apron off, I knew right away she didn't have sleeping on her mind.

I followed close behind her to the front room where Mr. Warren still had Mama cornered and was still trying to kiss her. He was so excited that he didn't hear Grandma come up behind him. Grandma was a firm believer in making sure you could see and hear what was going on for yourself before you took action. It didn't take her but one good, "Aw, come on, Nellie" to make her decision that what I told her was the Gospel.

With the force of all her 300 pounds behind her, she took her thumb and those two fingers and grabbed Mr. Warren's overalls right where the gallus straps crossed in the back. She slung him so hard against the front door that it knocked him out. Before he could fall to the floor, she pinned him up against the door with her stomach. When she grabbed the claw hammer right out of his loop, I closed my eyes. I had seen her hit a mad dog with a hammer and it was not a sight I wanted to see again. All I could think of was that if Mr. Warren had been a painter, the blood would have shown up better.

But instead of hitting him, she took five ten-penny nails from his nail pouch. With two of them, she hammered each gallus strap to the door. Then she grabbed his britches legs and nailed both of them to the door. She took the last nail, muscled up, and nailed the crotch of his overalls to the door. The banging sound was bringing Mr. Warren around, but when he saw that hammer headed between his legs, he passed out again. She turned him loose and there he hung.

She told me to go get her new brush broom from the car shelter. She broke her old one over Cousin Wayne for Cousin Coreen. On the way back through the house, I picked up her Bible and took it to her 'cause I knew she was going to need that, too. She took Mama by the arm and held her for just a minute, trying to calm her down. Then she handed Mama the newly made brush broom. Mama walked up to Mr. Warren hanging there on the door and said, "This is going to hurt you more than it is me." She stepped back and took a swing that had been handed down to her by Old Slugger herself. I saw Grandma swell up with pride.

Mr. Warren winced for the wallop he was about to receive, but Mama stopped the brush broom about one inch from his nose. He opened his eyes in disbelief and let out a sigh of relief. Mama got right in his sweating face and told him never to ever think about touching her again. Still shaking, she turned and handed the brush broom to Grandma and walked on into the kitchen. Grandma stared at him, then looked back at Mama and waited till she was out of sight. She asked me to go close the kitchen door. As I turned to go close the door, I heard a swishing sound followed by a hard, solid slap. I didn't see anything, I only heard it. I looked back and Grandma was still holding the brush broom, just like

Mama had given it to her. The right side of Mr. Warren's face had a red handprint on it. I always knew that if Grandma would unfold those other three fingers, she could change the course of the world. She told Mr. Warren her new brush broom was for sweeping dirt, not cow manure.

She walked toward Mr. Warren and he fainted again. This time, she took hold of the doorknob and slammed the door, swinging Mr. Warren outside the house. Cousin Wayne was walking by and saw Mr. Warren suspended above the porch. He threw down his liquor bottle and stumbled in a hurry back to his house. Grandma left Mr. Warren hanging there and went on back to the kitchen, put her apron back on, and started cleaning up her canning mess.

About two hours later, Cousin Wayne came back over to see if what he had seen was for real or was it his liquor playing tricks on him. Mr. Warren asked him to take his crowbar and pry the nails loose from his gallus straps. They got the straps loose and the nails in his britches legs out, but they couldn't figure out how to angle the crowbar to get the nail out of his crotch. Cousin Wayne took his Barlow knife out and cut the crotch out of Mr. Warren's overalls and cut him down. Mr. Warren left without his car or his tools. He must have come back during the night because they were gone the next morning when we got up.

Grandma let that patch of denim crotch hang on our door long enough for every do-gooder man in the village to hear about it or see it with his own eyes. My bed was in the front room and for weeks cars would ride by real slow at night and turn around out under the streetlight so that the headlights of the car would shine on the cloth on the door. When Grandma finally took it down, she told me and my sisters about the Passover story in the Bible. Even though we were young, we knew what message Grandma was sending out.

Me and Grandma had to finish our porch, but nobody ever bothered Mama again.

NEIGHBORHOOD WATCH

Most of the Mill Village houses were built very close to each other, usually separated by only a ditch or volunteer hedgerow. Since there was not a lot to do in the village, I got real good at sitting in the cedar tree in the front yard or the black walnut tree in the backyard, watching and listening to our neighbors. I could hear Cousin Wayne cuss and swear at Cousin Coreen and the young'uns. I could tell when he was drunk by how loud he got. The drunker he was, the louder he got. He always wanted out of what he called *This Hellhole*. I didn't know if he meant the house, his marriage, the village, or what. Grandma said the war had something to do with his drinking and swearing. She said his *Hellhole* was the memories he carried from seeing all the fighting and killing in the war firsthand. From the way he swore and got violent, I was glad he was on our side.

If Cousin Wayne was sober, I could watch Mrs. McLendon hang out her clothes. I could guess down to the last pair of cotton panties just exactly where she would spread her legs to pee and never miss a clothespin. I wasn't sure why she ever had to wash her bloomers, as it seemed she never wore any. I guess washing them made people think she did. She let those big drawers hang out long after she took her corset and slip in.

If I missed Mrs. McClendon's wash day, I could look across our garden and see if Mr. Bill and Mrs. Opal had anything going. It was fun to watch them cut each other's hair, and then take turns cutting their son Raymond's. Mr. Bill would try and hold Raymond down while Mrs. Opal cut, or shingled it, as Grandma would say.

Pulling a plow made Mrs. Opal real strong. When it was her turn to hold Raymond, she got around behind him and took her right foot—still with her shoe on—and put it right in the middle of Raymond's back. She grabbed both his arms and pulled them back behind him till they almost touched. It had to be a wrestling hold. Mrs. Opal had to use that hold on Raymond because he was seventeen years old, weighed 285 pounds, and hated to get his haircut.

But the most fun I had while looking at my neighbors was watching the Phillips family across the street. Mr. Phillips was a short, stout man. He always wore overalls and a flannel shirt, even in the summertime. He had the loudest sneeze I ever heard. I couldn't wait for spring each year for two reasons: baseball spring training, and watching the new pollen work on Mr. Phillips' hay fever.

Mrs. Phillips made Mr. Phillips stay outside because she couldn't stand the noise. When he sneezed, he gripped both gallos straps with his thumbs and reared back on his heels. His big belly pushed up onto his chest, and he let loose a sneeze that sounded like *AH SHAW!* After several *ah shaws*, his big belly fell out of his chest and settled back down, stretching the lower part of his bib overalls. He then took out a red and white cowboy-looking handkerchief and blew his nose so hard his old felt hat slid backwards several inches. After he put his handkerchief back in his pocket, he tilted his head forward, gripped the rear brim with his left hand, pulling it back and down. With his right hand, he pulled the front of the brim forward and down. It made him look just like a state trooper after you got pulled over for speeding. Mr. Phillips would have made a good state trooper based on hat adjustment alone.

Mr. Phillips sneezed one time and broke three of Mrs. Eunice's ribs, even though she was standing four feet away. They had a son named Howard who wore overalls too. He was a big man and had a real slow, deliberate walk. He had a nose that grew flat on his face, but other than that, he was a good-looking young man. My buddy Donald said maybe he was standing behind a door as a young'un when Mr. Phillips sneezed.

Mrs. Phillips was a frail woman who didn't get out of the house much, except when Mr. Phillips stayed in during the spring. It did give her time to work in her flower bed.

Probably my favorite part of the Phillips family was their son Terry. At about age fourteen, Terry decided he wanted to be a preacher. They were Methodists, but that was okay according to Grandma. Terry walked around and around their shotgun house, toting his Bible, looking down as he walked, and reading out loud. After he got tired of walking, he got up on their front porch, laid his Bible on the rail, and preached to the top of his lungs.

Cousin Wayne lived across the street from the Phillips and it made him real nervous when Terry preached from his front porch. If Cousin Wayne was sober, he would go inside. But if he was drunk, he would sit out in his old metal porch chair—the one that looked like it was made from an old Shell Oil sign—and holler *AMEN* every once in a while. It never seemed to bother Terry, as the louder Cousin Wayne got with his *amens*, the louder Terry preached.

If anybody walked by on the road, Cousin Wayne staggered out with his hat in his hand and took up an offering. Nobody ever refused, as they all knew just how violent Cousin Wayne could be. After Terry finished preaching, Cousin Wayne walked over and gave Terry half of the collection. This went on for years. Between Terry's preaching, Cousin Wayne's *amens*, and the collection, it was possible for Terry to go to seminary on his half of the money. Cousin Wayne used his half to buy himself a beer joint.

NOT A GOOD YEAR
FOR GRANDDADDY

Granddaddy was not one to work around our house. He didn't have to. Grandma did it all. Granddaddy said watching Grandma work really hard made him tired. That explained why he slept so much. Grandma stayed busy doing something all the time. She never sat down to rest and he never got up to work. They made a good husband and wife team.

Granddaddy's favorite place to rest was in an old multi-colored chenille hammock that hung on a green metal frame in the shade of the black walnut tree in the backyard. Granddaddy stood about five feet tall and those little short legs of his caused him a lot of trouble. When he tried to get in his hammock, he never could make it on his first try. He backed up to the side of the hammock, got on his tiptoes, leaned back, and slung his right leg up and over. He got just enough of his behind on the outside edge of the hammock to get what he thought was a grip, but it flipped him to the ground every time. I sat above him in the tree and watched him try every way he could think of to get in without falling out. All he had to do was call Grandma and she could pick him up and set him in it. But he didn't want to interfere with her work.

Cousin Wayne got to feeling sorry for Cousin Lee, as he called Granddaddy, and came over drunk one day with a plan to get Granddaddy safely in the hammock. Cousin Wayne had taken the door off Mr. Joe Dean's outhouse—with Mr. Joe still in it. He was a drinking buddy and told him it was for a good cause. Next, he tore down one of Grandma's chicken coops and used the wood to build something resembling a scaffold, similar to the ones the workers used when the mill had our house painted one year. He took a plowline that Mr. Smith left when he broke our garden in the spring and made a wind-up contraption—sort of like a well windlass—and nailed it to the top of the scaffold. He nailed the hinges of the outhouse door to the windlass frame. He tied a big double knot about four and a half feet up a length of rope, then tied a big loop at the other end.

He pulled enough rope off and had Granddaddy hold onto the knot and step in the loop. Cousin Wayne cranked the handle of the windlass and Granddaddy began to lift slowly off the ground. Back and forth. Back and forth. After he got Granddaddy higher than the hammock, he swung him over it as close to the center as he could. Granddaddy held onto the knot until Cousin Wayne eased him right on down into the hammock.

Cousin Wayne stayed drunk enough that Granddaddy talked him into singing him to sleep. Granddaddy knew he knew a lot of songs off his beer joint jukebox. Cousin Wayne leaned back against the old walnut tree and sang Granddaddy's favorite song, Carroll County Accident. When he finished that, he tried to sing all fifteen verses of Barbara Allen. Cousin Wayne always went to sleep before Granddaddy did and Granddaddy would finish it up for him. After they both had a good nap, they simply reversed the process and Granddaddy got safely back on the ground in no time.

One day Cousin Wayne came over as drunk as I had ever seen him. Granddaddy stepped in the loop and Cousin Wayne wound him up as high as he could and let go of the handle. Down Granddaddy came. Just as he hit the hammock, Cousin Wayne cranked the handle and up he went, right back to the top. He cranked and let go over and over. Granddaddy was holding on for what little life he had left. Up he went, down he came. His pocket watch slipped out of that little pocket slit in the front of his khakis. When Granddaddy started up, the watch started down. When

Granddaddy went down, the watch passed him on the way up. It looked like a yo-yo. Cousin Wayne was hollering, "What time is it, Cousin Lee? What time is it?" Prince Albert flew out of his pocket on the third trip down. His see-through green mechanical pencil that never had any lead in it fired out of his shirt pocket up into the black walnut tree.

Across the street at Mr. Morris's store, three of Granddaddy's Sunday school members, all in their seventies, were watching Mr. Lee jump up and down. They could not see the well rope or Cousin Wayne for the lower tree limbs. The next Sunday before church started, they asked Granddaddy how he learned to jump that high and why was he doing it. He said he was tired of picking up walnuts off the ground so he just jumped up and picked them off the tree. I don't think they listened to his Sunday school lesson much after that.

After several years, Granddaddy finally learned how to get in the hammock by himself. He got a running start, threw his leg over, twisted his body, landed flat on his back, and grabbed both sides of the hammock. He said he learned to do it while watching the high jump event in the Olympics on the television at O.K. Vaughn's Furniture Store while Grandma was in there paying her monthly bill.

One summer morning as Granddaddy lay in his hammock and I sat in my tree, something huge appeared in the sky back over behind the church. It was a large cigar-shaped thing that made a low humming sound. It looked like it was just sitting there. I climbed down the tree and got over beside Granddaddy, careful not to shake the hammock. I leaned over and whispered for him to wake up. Granddaddy pushed the front of his hat up over his eyes. He just lay there, eyes fixed on that thing up over the church.

Granddaddy told me to go get Cousin Wayne and ask him if he could see it too. He said to make sure he was drunk because the drunker he was the better he saw. He knew that for a fact because when Cousin Wayne came home from the beer joint, if he was not real drunk, he pulled his old Buick up near the front of his car shelter and stopped on the outside. But if he was real drunk, he turned it in the driveway and drove right into his car shelter at the same speed he left the road.

I couldn't find Cousin Wayne, so I went to find Grandma. She would know what it was. I couldn't find her, so I went across the road to Mr. Phillips' house to find Terry, their preacher-to-be son. The only one home was Mr. Phillips. I could see him asleep on the settee, but I couldn't get him to come to the door. He snored as loud as he sneezed. I went back over to Granddaddy and told him I couldn't find anybody. He started crying and carrying on, louder than I've ever heard him, except maybe the time when Grandma pulled all of his teeth. I asked him why he was crying and he hugged me up to him and said that surely he had slept through Gabriel's horn and that thing had to be all the Christians in the village being carried off to Glory.

He got out of his hammock, tears streaming down his face. He took his old wrinkled hands—always mottled with dark bruises on the backs of them—and put them on my shoulders. He said he could understand why he wasn't on it. He confessed to me about making moonshine one year without Grandma knowing. He made up a story about how the Lord would send back for me just as soon as He had put all the adults out and gave each of them a job to do. I think the thing that bothered him most was that Cousin Wayne made it and he didn't. I asked him, "Could it be that God knows He has to keep everybody in drinking water up there and He needs somebody that knows how to operate a well windlass?"

About that time, Mr. Phillips came over and sneezed that god-awful *Ah Shaw* of his about four good times right in our faces. Granddaddy looked at me and we both agreed that it would be hell to be left alone here with Mr. Phillips and his sneezing. We stood there still looking at the thing in the sky when Mama, Grandma, my sisters, and the rest of the Phillips family pulled up in the yard in our old Plymouth. Me and Granddaddy couldn't believe what we were seeing! We just knew that Grandma would have been in the first load to Glory.

Mama came over and said, "What do you think of the blimp?" She said Jim Hardin on WCOH radio station in Newnan said the Goodyear Tire and Rubber Company had built a blimp and it was flying from Newnan to Carrollton today. I told her I hoped it didn't run into the Glory Ship. She lifted up the front of my hair to see if 666 was on my forehead.

We all got tired of watching it and went on in the house, except Granddaddy. Even though by now he saw the word Goodyear printed in big black letters on the side of the thing, he still wasn't fully convinced that it wasn't really the Glory Ship. He waved and waved at it just to let them know where he was; he wasn't taking no chances.

Grandma had dinner fixed, which was what villagers called the noon meal. We ate breakfast, dinner, and supper in the Mill Village. City folks ate breakfast, lunch, and dinner. Grandaddy didn't come in to eat. It was not like him to miss a meal. He was not in his hammock or anywhere in the yard. The afternoon passed and so did the blimp.

When it came time for supper, Granddaddy was still nowhere to be found. Me and Grandma divided up the Mill Village. She took C, D, E, and F Streets and I went to A and B Streets to look for him. The whole village was notified that Mr. Lee had disappeared. Burvin went and rang the church bell. The men of the village gathered up and started helping us look for Granddaddy.

Dark fell and still no Granddaddy. Women came to sit with Grandma. His Sunday school class came and built a fire in the ditch in front of our house and stood around telling stories about Granddaddy, talking about him like he was gone for good. I remembered I hadn't seen Bullet the whole day either. I knew Granddaddy would be all right if *Bullock*, as he called him, was with him. Bullock would not let anything bother Granddaddy.

Around 8:00, one of the men found Granddaddy's felt hat in the woods near the ballpark. The back of it was scratched up pretty bad. Even I was worried now, as Granddaddy never went without his hat.

About eleven, just as hope was fading, the deacon that bought his liquor in Sargent drove up with Bullet sitting in the front seat and Granddaddy sitting in the bed of the truck, leaning against the cab. He was all scratched up and bleeding and had cockleburs and beggar's lice all over him. The deacon opened the door and let Bullet out and he looked as bad as Granddaddy.

Grandma went to the truck, cradled Granddaddy, and lifted him out. As she stood there holding him, she had me take out his folding wallet with the silver chain clipped to his belt loop, like the Merita Bread man toted. She told me to give Deacon Ellis a dollar for gas money for bringing her man home. There wasn't any money in the wallet. The only thing in it was the picture of the good-looking woman that was in the wallet when he bought it, the emergency notification card—still blank, his social security card, Masonic Lodge card, VFW card, and folded up in the secret pocket was the name and address of a glass jug and sugar wholesaler. Holding Granddaddy with just one arm, Grandma reached in her bosom bra and pulled out her handkerchief with the money in it. She untied the knot with those two fingers of hers, took out a dollar bill, and gave it to Deacon Ellis.

She toted Granddaddy to the porch and asked him where he had been for so long. He said he was standing there watching the blimp and to him, it looked real close and slow-moving. He saw the word Goodyear on it and just knew there had to be something written on the other side. So he struck out to walking, trying to get to the other side to read what it said. He told her he gave out between Sargent and Whitesburg and never did get around to the other side of it. He said Bullet ran on ahead and he thinks he did get to the other side, but since he couldn't read or talk, it didn't do either one of them any good. He said Deacon Ellis picked them up on their way back through Sargent.

Grandma looked down at Bullet and thanked him for staying with Granddaddy. She looked at Granddaddy, hugged him real tight, and said, "Ain't he pitiful." She carried him on in the house, bathed him, doctored his scratches with Tincture Merthiolate, and rocked him to sleep in her big cane bottom chair, singing all fifteen verses of Barbara Allen.

SHE CAN'T PLAY. PERIOD!

Growing up in the Mill Village, I learned about life in many different ways. Most things I learned came directly from Grandma. Some things came from my buddy Donald. Other things I learned on my own. I think as a boy you are born with boy things already locked away in your brain. When things happen that only a boy should know, something inside your brain tells you, *I know about that because I am a boy.* The first time I ever had my picture made, the cameraman had Mama roll me a ball with red, white, and blue stars on it. When the ball rolled between my legs, even though I was a baby, I looked down at that ball and knew right away to try and roll it back to Mama. I was a boy. I knew about playing ball.

God knew boys would love balls so much we came with two factory-installed—most of us, anyway. An assistant principal of mine had only one. We called him Squirrel because he was only carrying one nut. I never figured out how everybody found out he just had one ball or *gland* as Grandma made me call them. I guessed it had to be the doctor that delivered him, but Donald said it couldn't have been him as doctors take a hypodermic oath or some secret-sounding thing like that, sort of like the Masons.

Another buddy of mine had three glands. That was fact because he was so proud of them he showed them to anybody, anywhere, anytime. He had a little old hose, but with three glands I guess it would have been just too much to ask for him to be blessed all the way around. We nicknamed him Tri-cod. Of course, Grandma made me call him *Tri-glands*. Tri-glands was the catcher for our Mill Village baseball team. Wilson Sporting Goods had to special make him a catcher's cup to protect all of him. When he quit playing, his mother had his catcher's cup bronzed and put it up on the mantle next to his baby shoes.

I couldn't wait for the warm weather of spring to come; it meant the beginning of ball season. We played baseball in the Mill Village, but only after hours *if* you made the team. Arnco-Sargent School didn't have a basketball gym, the ropes on our tetherball poles stayed broken thanks to Big Bobby Burnham, and Mill Village boys had never seen a for-real football. The girls played kickball with soft, smelly, red rubber balls—not a true red, but a dull red, sort of like the sweeping compound the janitors used on our lunchroom floors. The balls had a finish on them just like the swimming caps I saw some of the city girls wear one day when me and Grandma walked by the Newnan City Pool on our way down to Pickett Field to watch our Mill Village team play a road game.

And us boys? During recess, we had to play *softball*. I hated kickball, but I hated softball even worse. A traveling salesman came to the Mill Village one year and tried to sell the mill team a box of softballs. I remember the coach calling him a *queer* and made us young'uns get in the dugout until Lester Melear's son-in-law, the mill team's big first baseman, stuffed him back in his rolling store. We never saw him. I knew what a *queer* was because I was a boy and boys knew about that word.

One day at recess, just as me and Tommy Farrell were about to pick sides for our softball game, Mr. Jones, our new principal, came out and said that he thought it would be nice if we let the girls play. *Girls?* Playing *softball?* Who ever heard of such a thing? We pitched a fit and gave him all sorts of reasons why they shouldn't play. First off, for some reason, they can't throw overhanded. I told him if you put a girl in the outfield and the ball is hit near her, even if she finally does stop it, I don't care how far away she is, she will try to throw it to you underhanded. I know, I saw girls try and throw back foul balls we hit on their kickball field.

Always underhanded. I told him sometimes they held onto it for too long and then swung their arms wild and threw it *behind* them. They could accidentally hurt some of our star baseball players that way. Tommy told him that they couldn't slide or they might mess up their dress or crinoline. And those slick bottom black patent leather shoes sure weren't running shoes either. I also told him they didn't always know which base to run to, from what I saw of them playing kickball. If they ever did happen to get on base, they wouldn't know when to tag up on a fly ball and they'd never get straight to run on anything with two outs. They wouldn't know how to call for fly balls and some of us boys might run into them. We could lose some of our best outfielders by them twisting something trying to keep from running over a girl. It wasn't their fault. They just weren't born with any ball knowledge. Because they weren't boys.

Mr. Jones made it clear that if the girls couldn't play softball, then the boys couldn't play softball. Instead, he said we would all have to play with those soft, smelly, red rubber balls. We didn't have a choice. None of us boys would ever get to play on the Mill Village team if the men found out we had played kickball with those smelly balls.

The only girl in the whole school that I thought might come close to playing softball was a girl named Joan. She was sort of a tomboy. I had my eye on her. In order to see who got to choose first, me and Tommy walked our hands up the bat to see who would come out on top; whoever's hand capped the end of the bat got to choose first. Tommy won. We took turns until all the good players were picked, and then all the rest of the boys. Even the worst boy had to be better than a girl.

I got the first turn to choose a girl. All of us were crowded around home plate except Joan; she was leaning up against the end of the school building. I pointed over to her and said, "I choose

Joan." She just stood there. I pointed again and yelled her name and motioned for her to come on. "You're holding up the choosing," I told her. The game hadn't even started yet and already a girl was ruining it. Joan called one of her friends over and whispered something to her. I hollered again for her to come on. Her friend came over and told me that Joan couldn't play—that she was sick. I said she didn't look sick and begged her to please come on.

Mrs. Wortham, my teacher, walked over to Joan and whispered in her ear. Had I done something wrong that made her not want to play on my team? I couldn't remember doing anything to her in school, in fact, I was a little afraid of her and always tried to be nice to her. She was bigger than I was. I told Tommy to take her. Tommy hollered if she didn't want to play on my team it was all right, she could be on his. Mrs. Wortham came over and told us both to choose somebody else—that Joan was indeed sick. I looked at Mrs. Wortham and told her again, "Joan don't look sick. If she was a boy, you'd make her play." Mrs. Wortham took me off to the side and whispered to me that Joan was on her period and therefore could not play.

Nothing in my boy-mind clicked. I wasn't sure what it meant, but I didn't want to let on, just in case it was a boy word. I told Mrs. Wortham that we all had just come from our fourth period and that now we were all at recess and when the bell rang again, we would all be in our fifth period, including Joan. She couldn't be on her period. She was on her recess. Mrs. Wortham told me again that Joan was sick and on her period. I hollered over to Joan and told her not to let that keep her from playing, that a few nights ago my Granddaddy had the same thing. She should take some Three S Tonic when she got home and she'd be just fine.

By now, everybody roared and laughed and carried on—all except Mr. Jones and Mrs. Wortham. I thought they were laughing because I really had told a good one, so I hollered one more time, "Yep, my Granddaddy's on his period a lot. Far as I know, he's the only one in the family that ever has it. Mama, Grandma, and my sisters never do get a case of it. Nope. Just Granddaddy."

My buddies started falling all over each other and holding their sides. I thought I was really on a roll! I told everybody, "Why just the other night I had to sleep with Granddaddy and I was afraid I'd catch a period from him, so I took two doses of Three S Tonic all by myself just to keep from getting it."

When Mr. Jones heard enough, he grabbed me up by my good ear and pulled me as far away from everybody as we could get. He proceeded to try and explain it to me, from Eve in the Garden of Eden to the sanitary belt factory in Newnan. I was one confused boy. This was definitely not boy stuff. For the first time in my life, I wished Donald or Grandma or somebody had told me about girl stuff.

Finally, Mr. Jones told me, "The best thing for you to do is, the next time y'all play ball and it's your turn to choose? If you happen to see a girl leaning up against the building? Don't choose her."

THE
GOATMAN

When I first started to school, it was a big step leaving the security of Mama's and Grandma's protective apron strings. It was easy to feel sorry for myself, sitting there on the first day surrounded by fidgeting, crying people I didn't even know. While I was eager to learn, I somehow thought that if Mrs. Jones would just let me go home, between Grandma and Mama, I could pick up enough of life's secrets to survive in the Mill Village. Eat, sleep, play ball, go to church, charge at the stores, and bathe on special occasions. I already knew those things. Surely there was not much left for me to know in order to get through life.

I already found the mention of my birth in Grandma's Bible. If she was still around when I passed on, she would record that in her Bible, too. To me, that's all I needed in order to get into heaven. I was a shoo-in to enter the Pearly Gates, so what did it matter what I did in between? How could book learning be that important? I asked Grandma why I had to go to school. She knew that if she told me it was to learn things, I was ready to tell her all about what I already knew. So that's not what she said. Grandma had a way of making you make a decision contrary to what you were thinking. But she did it in such a way that after you made the decision, you felt so good about it you thought it had been your idea all along.

Grandma told me Mrs. Jones' husband ran the dairy at their house up on the Newnan Highway and that he sold his milk to all the schools in Coweta County. She said that if I quit school, then some of my buddies might quit too, and if they quit, then somebody else might quit, and pretty soon all the schools in the county would be empty. She said poor Mrs. Jones would be out of a job and that Mr. Jones would not have anybody to sell his milk to and he and Mrs. Jones might lose their whole herd and maybe even their farm. I went back to school the next day. I told Mrs. Jones if I ever missed a day of school, not to worry. I would be back because I knew how important it was for her and Mr. Jones to work.

First grade was pretty dull. Alice and Jerry. Dick and Jane and Spot. They all seemed too fake for me. I listened pretty good in class and not once did anything I read about in Dick and Jane take place at school. At recess, when we played ball for the first time, my new buddy Tommy hit the ball and ran to first base. I listened while he ran. Not once did anybody say, "See Tommy run. Run, Tommy, run! Look, Lawrence, look!"

I went home talking like Dick and Jane one day. I went in and told Grandma, "Look, Grandma, look! See Cousin Wayne chase Bullet. Run, Bullet, run! See Cousin Wayne stagger. Look, Grandma, look. See Cousin Wayne fall." I talked that way the whole evening. It got Grandma so aggravated that she took me out on the back porch and said, "See the razor strap. See Lawrence jump! Jump, Lawrence, jump!" I shut up right then and Grandma went on back to the kitchen mumbling that if I kept on talking that way, she didn't care if Mr. and Mrs. Jones did have to sell their dairy.

Mrs. Jones did everything she could to make school fun for us. She showed us how to make turkeys out of colored paper and pine cones. Not little green pine cones, but the big ones that were opened out all the way. We always had to pick up the pine cones in the principal's yard, right next to the schoolyard. There were plenty of pine trees in our schoolyard, but Mrs. Jones said the cones from our principal's yard were a special kind, just right for making turkeys. They all looked the same to me.

We had a man from the forest service come to our class one day to teach us all about nature and different kinds of leaves and trees. Anytime we had a special guest, the principal would come and sit in with our class. During the question and answer time with the forest service man, I asked him why the pine trees in our principal's yard were different than the ones in our schoolyard. The principal and Mrs. Jones squirmed. The man said the trees were all the same and that there was no difference. Mrs. Jones sprung up and thanked the man for his time. He interrupted that he was not quite finished. She responded with, "Oh yes you are." I could tell that we had just made turkeys again, but this time without the pine cones.

Things got real slow after that. Even at recess the traffic going from Newnan to Carrollton didn't seem as heavy as it once did. I thought they must have had some layoffs at Plant Yates, the local Georgia Power Company. Traffic did pick up once that year when the train derailed in Whitesburg. None of us had ever seen a train derail, except in the papers, so they let us go see. Anne, the only girl in our class that had a television, said she had seen one on the Six O'clock News one time, so she was the only one in our class that did not go to see the wreck. School let out early so all the teachers could go see the train wreck so maybe they might prepare some new current event related classroom material for us. The principal and Mrs. Jones stayed behind to pick up the ever-increasing number of pine cones in the principal's yard, since we had quit making turkeys.

One day, Mrs. Jones said she had a special surprise for us. At ten a.m. the whole school let out and we marched in single file by grades to the hill overlooking the Carrollton Highway. The hill was where I would stand before school each day and wait for Mrs. Jones to drive by in her big old DeSoto. I loved to watch all those blinker lights on the tail end of that car. That model had a big chrome grill and big long fins in the rear that had the lights stacked on top of each other—red on top, clear in the middle, and red again on the bottom. I had never seen so many taillights on a car.

The taillights never worked on the car we had. Mama always had to stick her arm out straight for left turns and bent up in an L shape to turn right. Mrs. Jones' DeSoto did not have a gear shift lever like the rest of the cars. It just had buttons mounted on the dash to push for whatever gear you wanted. Of all the fancy parts on the car, I still liked the taillights best. I told Grandma about the car and how much I liked the blinking lights and she told me she hoped when I got old I would stay out of beer joints. She had a meaning for everything she said.

We were all standing lined up on the hill waiting for whatever it was that we had been sent out there to see. I looked to my left towards Sargent and saw a contraption slowly making its way for us. As it got closer, I saw what I thought was a bunch of animals pulling two wood and tin covered carts with big steel wheels. Walking along behind were even more of those animals, whatever they were. Beside the lead cart was a mountain of a man dressed in overalls, blue jean jacket, no shirt, and brown ankle-high work boots. He had a full beard and long shaggy black hair. The odor reached us before he got within a hundred yards of us. As he got closer, I thought surely what I was seeing had to be someone Noah had left off the ark. It seemed whoever this person was and whatever those animals were had escaped the flood somehow and had been looking for old Noah to ask why they were left off.

The old carts had hubcaps, pots, pans—anything that he found on the roadside that the goats were too full to eat—hanging on the sides of them. The carts must have weighed more than the boxcar loads of coal I had seen outside Plant Yates. Creaking and clanking and thumping and shaking every time the steel wheels rolled over the tar dividers on the concrete highway, the animal-powered cart finally made its way up to us and stopped at the foot of the hill.

The man looked to be in his fifties. He took a red and white handkerchief from his back pocket, blew his nose, then wiped his brow with it. After looking from the nose of the first animal to the tale of the last and the two carts in between, I realized I had come face-to-face with The Goatman. I heard Mama and Grandma talking about him one time, about how he travels all over the south with his goats. His choice of goats to pull his carts seems real smart to me, as they would eat anything along the highway, didn't need much water, and he could drink their milk. Our principal introduced him as The Goatman and apologized for not having a gift or something for him. My buddy Woody stepped behind me and hollered down, "Why don't you give him a pine cone turkey?" Mrs. Jones snatched him up and sent him running back to the schoolhouse.

The Goatman stood there and preached to us about everything from the creation to the second coming of the Lord—something us Baptists talked about a lot. He then showed us some of his prized goats. He said he would give a dollar to anyone that could ride his biggest male goat. Joan, the tomboy in our class, jumped off the hill and landed right on top of that goat. She rode him all over the side of the hill. When she was done, she rode right to The Goatman and hopped off with her hand out. The Goatman said he never had anybody ride that goat before. He leaned over to our principal and asked him if he could borrow a dollar.

The Goatman thanked us for letting him stop to visit and then prayed the longest and most sincere-sounding prayer I had heard since Uncle Seabron prayed at our last family reunion. If Grandma thought Uncle Seabron was going to pray at reunions, she would always let her food stay on the stove a little longer than usual. The Goatman prayed for all of us young'uns to grow up to be good women and gentlemen and he prayed that we would always do right and never cuss or talk ugly to anybody. He finished it off with a triple amen. I couldn't wait till Sunday to tell Mr. Jackson so he might try a triple amen himself and impress all the other deacons. The head of our lunchroom ladies had gone back to the school during his prayer and brought The Goatman a sack of rolls for him to take with him.

The Goatman thanked us again for coming out to see him, waved goodbye, and hollered for his goats to get up. He didn't notice that one of them had gone to sleep behind the back wagon. As he started off, one of the heavy steel wheels rolled over the goat's leg. It bleated a blood-curdling bleat. The Goatman spun around on the rubber heel of his boot and ran back toward the goat, yelling, "Ya damn morphodite!" The goat's leg was bleeding pretty bad. He took some kerosene, poured it on his handkerchief, and wrapped it around the goat's leg. Throwing the goat up in the back of the wagon, he headed on down the Carrollton Highway.

When we got back in the classroom, I asked Mrs. Jones just what kind of goat a *damn morphodite was*. She shifted in her chair, looked anxiously from side to side, and saw the whole class waiting for her to answer. She calmly stood up and told us that the markings on the goat and the size of the horns on its head distinguished it as a Morphodite goat. She said they were rare and most people didn't recognize one when they saw it and that's why we probably had never heard of them before. She said that if somebody heard he had one, they might try to knock The Goatman in the head and steal it from him. She said for us please not to tell anybody about what we were talking about, not even our parents.

After meeting The Goatman, I thought he was surely a learned man; traveling and getting to go places and see things made him an educated man to me. I wanted to grow up to live like that and be like him. That would get me out of the Mill Village.

A few weeks later, Uncle Shorty took Grandma, my sisters, and me to the Coweta County Fair. Grandma took my sisters to the women places at the fair. They liked the canning section, the quilt section, and stuff that only women like to look at. Uncle Shorty took me to the livestock exhibit. We walked from stall to stall looking at all the prized animals that the local FFA members had brought to show off. A large crowd was gathering for the final judging of the animals. Lo and behold, as we moved to take our seats, we passed what had to be the finest looking goat I have ever seen. I looked at him real hard. I could just see it being the lead goat on my goat train.

As me and Uncle Shorty stood there and looked at the goat, our preacher and his wife came up and started talking to Uncle Shorty. The preacher looked down at me and ran his hand over the top of my head and asked me if I was having a good time at the fair. I told him how happy I was that Uncle Shorty had taken the time off from running his store to bring us. The preacher's wife looked down at me and asked me which of the animals I liked best. I had already surveyed the markings on the goat in front of us, so I rocked back on my heels and said in a loud, proud voice, "Of all the animals," I paused and pointed through the fence, "the one I like best of all is that damn morphodite goat over there." Uncle Shorty froze. I realized how startled and amazed they must have been to see firsthand that a little first grader knew about the rare morphodite goat. So again, I said, "Yep, that's about the best looking damn morphodite goat I've ever seen. I can't wait to tell Mrs. Jones about seeing another one, since she was the one that told me all about 'em."

Mrs. Jones quit her teaching job the next week and went to work with her husband at the dairy.

PICKLED FEET AND PICKLED TOES

Women in the Mill Village were the best cooks in the world. They were not fancy cooks, just cooks. Whatever they cooked always tasted as good as it looked and you could always tell what it was. I hadn't seen fancy cooks before until I went to a wedding in Newnan. Most of the food couldn't be identified. When they served it to you, there was more plate than food. They would put an uncooked piece of green plant leaf somewhere on the plate. Grandma always told us to eat everything on our plate, that if we didn't, it might hurt the feelings of the one that had prepared it. I always tried to, including the uncooked green plant leaf. Grandma went to a wedding in Newnan one year. When she came back home, she changed the rules about eating everything on your plate. She said if it was city cooking you were facing, that rule no longer applied.

When we had all day sings with eating, I made sure I knew where Grandma and Mama put their basket of food. We had an old brown straw picnic basket that came with colorful hard plastic plates, knives, forks, spoons, and cups. There was also an old collapsible aluminum cup that I loved to drink out of. The aluminum made whatever you were drinking seem a lot colder than if you drank the same thing out of a plastic cup. After you drank from the aluminum cup, you smashed the top of it and it mashed flat as a flitter. I never knew what a flitter was. Donald said he thought it was supposed to be *flat as a fritter*, like those flat cornbread fritters Grandma cooked on top of the stove in our old iron skillet. They look like pancakes, only they're made out of cornmeal. Donald said the saying originated over here in the

United States, but that the Japanese got a hold of it during the war, and since they get their 'l's and 'r's mixed up, it came out like flitter. It made sense to me. Boy, that Donald knew more than anybody in the Mill Village, except Grandma.

When you opened the top of our picnic basket, there was a gathered elastic band stapled across the top to hold the forks, knives, and spoons. Grandma replaced the matching colored plastic utensils with metal ones, so as not to lose them or have someone pick them up by mistake. With a horseshoe nail, she scratched the initials B and C on each one of them—for the first initials of our last names: Bledsoe and Cole. They were the only set of monogrammed utensils in the Mill Village. The only other thing that even came close to a monogram was the tattoo on Cotton Smith's arm.

There are certain things as a young'un you learn not to like when it comes to eating. Mill Village young'uns are born hating liver, chitlins, broccoli, cooked carrots, and those little round green peas. Alvin Cash was the only young'un in the village that ate the little round green peas. He said they reminded him of tender young chinaberries.

Mr. Morris, Mr. Harris, and Uncle Shorty all sold stuff in their stores that us boys learned we had to eat in order to become men. We had only seen men eat these things, so we just assumed they were for men only. At each store, on top of the glass front counters, always near the old manual brass cash register, sat four large, bluish glass jars. They were arranged from left to right in order of how good they were. The far-left jar had whole pickles, the next had whole pickled boiled eggs, and the third had hot smoked beef jerky.

One day, Cotton Smith brought a poor as bones stolen cow to our house. He told me and Donald that he was not feeding the cow on purpose so that the meat would shrivel up and he could sell the cow for beef jerky on the hoof. The cow died before Cotton could sell it.

The last jar on the countertop had pickled pigs' feet in it. There were always strings of the pork hanging down off the feet. I could eat the whole pickles and eggs with no problem. I had to really work to eat the beef jerky, 'cause I kept on thinking about Cotton's poor old cow. But it took me years to even think about unscrewing the top off that pickled feet jar. I knew if I was to become a man, I would someday have to eat one. Donald said it was in the Bible somewhere.

There was one person in the Mill Village that I thought of every time I saw a jar of pickled pig's feet. James Gaddy lived in the first house on B Street, right next to the water tank just outside the fence that went around the mill. Mr. Gaddy was a hard worker when he got to work, but even though you could see the mill's smokestack and water tank from any street in the village, old James always had trouble finding the mill. He was a good man, a fine hand at the mill, but he had no sense of direction. Whatever direction his old Studebaker slat-side truck was pointed when he got in to go to work that morning, that was the direction he headed off in. Morning after morning, when he would not be in the weave shop at the start of his shift, his supervisor would go find his neighbor, Mrs. Mozley, and ask which direction the truck was pointed in that morning. That way he would at least know which direction to start looking. There were eight mills within twenty miles of our village and old James would drive till he saw one and then stop and go to work. Every once in a while he would show up at a mill that was short-handed that morning and they would let him work. Most times though, the mill guard would turn him around, point him toward Arnco and off he'd go. Old James did that so much he was voted most valuable employee at two different mills in one year.

Our mill finally realized that he was too good of an employee to fire, so they moved him to the house on B Street right next to the mill. They also borrowed a county road grader and fixed his driveway and put up One Way Only signs on both sides of the dirt-covered concrete culvert that turned from B Street into his yard. They got the convicts from the Newnan Work Camp to print up metal road signs that read:

ARNCO MILL STRAIGHT AHEAD

ARNCO MILL FIFTY FEET

YOU ARE APPROACHING ARNCO MILL

WORKPLACE OF JAMES GADDY

The warden at the Work Camp impounded a slick Yankee's car that had a compass on the dash. He had it removed and sent it to James for him to have mounted in his truck. A Mill Village supervisor's son—an Eagle Scout with a uniform and everything—taught him how to read the compass and gave him the return readings from any of the other eight mills, just in case he ever backed in his driveway to unload his lawnmower or groceries or something.

The mill had a sign company from Atlanta erect a large billboard in front of James's house that read ARNCO MILL DUE EAST. Some of James' fellow workers took old bricks from a torn down chimney at the old school and lay three rows of bricks out on his driveway all the way to the front of the weave shop. Along the three-brick private road were signs spaced about ten feet apart, sort of like the Burma Shave signs on the way to Carrollton. The signs read:

ATTENTION JAMES

IF YOU ARE READING THIS

YOU ARE DOING FINE

JUST FOLLOW THE ROW OF BRICKS

AND YOU'LL GET TO WORK ON TIME

THEN PARK AT YOUR PERSONAL PARKING PLACE

CUT OFF YOUR TRUCK

AND GO IN

DO THE SAME THING IN THE MORNING

AND YOU'LL FIND ARNCO MILL AGAIN

James was not only a good mill worker, but he also worked odd jobs trying to get his ends close together. Somehow they never seemed to meet. James had seen one of the Mill Village supervisors start letting grass grow in his yard where it had always been just dirt before. He figured the other supervisors would copy him and soon everybody would have grass growing. He knew that if he could ever cut one supervisor's yard, the others would never be caught cutting their own. So James set himself up in the lawn mowing business in the Mill Village.

Before people let grass grow, yards were all swept clean with a brush broom. I wondered why Grandma would ask me to sweep the yard clean when the very dirt I was sweeping was what I had to wash off me every other night to come clean. I knew yard dirt was dirt and dirt by nature was dirty, regardless if it was in a garden, in a flower box, or in a potted plant on the porch. Dirt gets even dirtier when you add water to it. Water cleans most everything else, but not dirt. It makes mud when you add water, and mud is dirtier than dirt. I had a real problem with that when I swept the yard. Even though Grandma would tell me when it looked good enough for her, I never felt like the yard was ever entirely clean.

I walked down to the mill one day to watch them paint the water tank. The sign on one of the trucks that was there to paint the tank said *Sandblasting*. I asked one of the workers what they used the sand for and he told me it helped clean the old paint off. Boy was I confused. I told him dirt didn't clean anything, but if you did try to use it, don't add water. He cussed me and went back to sandblasting. I figured cleaning with dirt was just one of those things in life that is put there to confuse you, like boiling water for tea, then cooling it with ice, then putting sugar in it to sweeten it, then putting lemon in to sour it up. Stuff like that.

James did not have a gas-powered mower, so he built one. He took four old sling blades, wedged them in between two old, hard rubber wheels, and attached a plow handle on a frame he built to make the wheels turn. When he pushed it, the blades rolled over and over with every turn of the wheel. It was the most awful piece of equipment you ever saw, but somehow the thing worked.

James went over to the ballpark and cut the grass that grew in the outfield. James came back and told his neighbors that his mower could cut down anything. His neighbor called his hand and bet him a can of Prince Albert—which was a considerable bet— that his mower would not cut kudzu. James told him he could cut all the kudzu that ran from the back of the church all the way over to the railroad tracks.

We all heard about the bet and turned out the Saturday morning of the cutting. Old James backed up to the curb on C Street, which was about 100 feet from the kudzu. Pushing barefooted—he never wore shoes, not even to work in the mill— he got a running start and took off across that churchyard. He pushed that homemade mower as fast as it would go, slinging rocks and dirt everywhere. He did not have a blade adjustment on his mower, the blades were just a bit higher than the ground.

He was at full speed when he hit the first set of vines just off the churchyard. He went about seventy-five feet into the kudzu and all we saw was vines trailing him and bare feet breaking through every once in a while. Then he would disappear again.

After he was about 300 feet into the thickest part of the kudzu, we heard James holler to the top of his lungs. The lawnmower, James, and the kudzu vines came to a halt. All got still. There wasn't the slightest ruffle of kudzu leaves.

After ten or fifteen minutes, the kudzu pile started creeping towards us. As it got closer, we realized that the sticky fluid that oozed out of the cut kudzu had glued all the loose leaves all over old James, making him look like one of my camouflage plastic army men. He fought his way out of the green tangle, pulling the mower behind him, and holding up something in his right hand. We couldn't see what it was for all the mess. It wasn't until he got out of the kudzu patch and walked over to us that we realized what he was holding. It was his big toe.

He walked straight over to his neighbor, who was holding his sides, rolling on the churchyard ground laughing. He told him he would have made it if the one-by-four wooden blade guard had not come off, causing his big toe to jam up the blade. The neighbor got up off the ground and handed James the can of Prince Albert. He earned it.

James pushed his mower across the street to our house where Grandma washed his foot with kerosene, then took a knitting needle and some colored nylon 100-pound test line and sewed up James's foot. She put his big toe in an empty pimento jar, filled it with alcohol, pressed the top back on, and gave it to James. He took it home and set it on his mantle. From time to time he took that jar out on the front porch where passersby could see it. Over the years, it began to get stringy, just like the pickled feet in those glass jars.

I saw that toe every time I started to reach for a pickled pig's foot. I just couldn't make myself take the top off that big jar. I either got the jerky or pickled eggs and went on back home, worrying I would stay in puberty for the rest of my life.

J. Rob Casey | 123

One day, I was at the store getting a Zero candy bar when James pulled up in his truck to get gas. He walked in, barefoot as usual, and after a few minutes came out drinking a Nehi Grape and eating, of all things, a pickled pig's foot. I knew if he could, I could. I walked over and asked him if he minded if I ate one with him, then ran back inside, swapped my Zero, and opened the fourth jar. Me and old James sat there on the bed of his truck and ate them down to the last knuckle.

As old James drove off, I thanked him. I walked back to the house knowing I was now ready to face manhood.

ALL-NIGHT SINGS
AND REVIVALS

Two things that us Baptists are quite fond of are all-day singings and revivals. It was announced in church one Sunday that on the fifth Sunday night of the next month, there would be an all-night singing, followed by a full week of revival. Preacher Edison announced we would have an evangelist hold the services for the entire week.

I asked Grandma what the difference was between a visiting preacher and an evangelist. She looked me in the eyes to see if I was sincere or if I was just making conversation. Grandma did not believe in wasting words on idle chitchat. I think she based that belief on the Bible scripture that says we will be held accountable for all the words we say. She knew if I ever did get to heaven, I probably could not stand still in front of the old Master long enough for Him to go over everything I had ever said.

After she determined I was sincere and just a young boy looking for answers to life's questions, she told me the differences. She said visiting preachers were usually from close by and most times had non-preaching full-time jobs. Their wives ironed their shirts for them; they wore black lace-up shoes, regardless of the color of their suit; they carried only one Bible, always drove a used car, and preached for a love offering.

She said evangelists preached all over the South and evangelizing was their full-time job. They had many suits with matching silk ties and kept a silk handkerchief in their coat pocket. Their shirts got starched at the laundry; they had slip-on shoes in different colors that they wore with thin see-through silk socks;

they had their britches hemmed short so they could show off their silk socks. They wore a lot of gold jewelry, got their hair cut, styled, and colored at a beauty shop, and most of them used hairspray. They carried Bibles printed in every available version. They had only three or four sermons because they traveled so often and preached somewhere different every week; chances of somebody hearing the same sermon twice was pretty rare. They handed out religious tracts with their statistics on them, like where they were from, where they went to school, what kind of preaching degrees they held, how many people they have preached to, how many people saved, and how many people that rededicated their lives. I asked her if religious tracts were sort of like baseball cards, and she said we would live to see it. She said they always drove a new car, usually foreign. She said they had all gone to a speech school that taught them how to make that *AH* sound after every word when they were preaching. They only came for a guaranteed amount of money and always brought 33 1/3, 45, and 78 RPM records to sell for profit in the church lobby. I didn't have to ask Grandma who she liked more, preachers or evangelists.

The all-night gospel sings never lasted all night. It sounded hypocritical for a church to announce it was having an all-night sing and then for it to not last all night. They usually started at seven and wrapped up around midnight. All-night sings usually began with the preacher welcoming everybody, then the choir director leading the entire congregation in a few songs from the hymnal. Since they never missed an opportunity to collect money, they always took up an offering.

One of the Mill Village supervisors had the only checking account in our church. He always made a big deal out of writing a big check every time the plate was passed. Instead of holding it up, he placed it signature-side up, so as the plate passed, everyone could see how much it was made out for. But he always got up and went to the back of the church after the offering. Grandma said if he wrote a check for twenty dollars, he would take eighteen dollars cash out of the plate, but it made him look like he gave the full twenty to the church. Grandma said when he had his taxes filed every year, it made him look like a very good church contributor, which helped him get a big refund. She said Uncle Sam may not know what was taking place, but God Almighty sure did, and that God's penalty was a lot worse than Uncle Sam's.

I asked her who Uncle Sam was and she said he was every American's uncle. I asked her, "Isn't Uncle Sam uncle to everybody else in the world, too?" She said, "No, just Americans." Confusion was a way of life for me. Baptists talk about everybody in the whole world being brothers and sisters, but if we were all brothers and sisters, how could Uncle Sam be uncle to Americans, but not to everybody else? She said he was uncle to folks who were born under the flag.

I remembered from Bible school that our church had two flags: a U.S. flag and a Christian flag. Now I had to figure out which flag she meant. I also knew about the flag they used at KKK rallies and the flag on the State Capitol building in Atlanta that I saw when we went to Grant Park Zoo. I thought about the flag on our mailbox. Cousin Weem was given a military funeral and he was buried under a flag, except even then they took it off and gave it to Aunt Blanche.

Grandma usually didn't talk in parables; you usually knew what she meant. But I could not figure out what she meant about being born under the flag. And I could not figure out who Uncle Sam was. Grandma told me not to worry till I was eighteen, then I would know who Uncle Sam was because he would want me. I hoped that Grandma would still be around when I turned eighteen because Uncle Sam would have one hell of a fight on his hands if he did show up to get me. I felt secure for the first time.

After the collection, the choir director introduced local church people to sing first. The guest singers—most times a trio or quartet—would sing next and get everybody in the spirit. The night of the gospel sing before the revival, we had a group called the Isom Lee Singers. They were from up near Fairburn, led by a man named Isom Lee, who was in his seventies, and his two daughters. Mr. Isom sang lead, one of his daughters sang alto, and the other sang soprano. Mr. Isom had the gift of getting people in the spirit real early on in the song service. He would lift his trembling hands up toward heaven and cry real tears on any song he wanted to. Almost everybody in the church would be squalling. The only time I ever cried was when I saw a tear rolling down Grandma's cheek. I figured she was thinking about her man again.

The church house was full; even Cousin Wayne was there and he had never been to anything at church before. Grandma told me she thought she saw Cousin Wayne get out of the car with the evangelist. The ladies were singing their hearts out when the evangelist came in from the vestibule where he had been setting his records up. He smelled a lot like Cousin Wayne to me. I looked up and saw that Grandma had smelled him too. So as not to interrupt the song service by going up on the podium, he just took a seat in a pew directly across the aisle from Cousin Wayne. Me and Grandma were sitting about eight rows back.

It was a hot, muggy night and the head of the building and grounds committee was in charge of seeing that everybody stayed as comfortable as they could. He gave out McKoon fans and opened all the windows. He propped the front doors open with two large rocks that have been used as door stops as long as the church has been there. Our old doors did not have those little kickstands near the bottom to hold them open.

On the last verse of a real crowd-moving song about Moses and Babylon, there was a commotion at the back of the church. A strong gust of hot summer wind slammed the doors shut. Just as Mr. Lee lifted his hands up and his girls were hollering to the top of their lungs, "God hewed out the rock that went rolling into Babylon," both door props came rolling down the aisle. One of the rocks stopped by Cousin Wayne's foot and the other stopped right by the evangelist's. Grandma whispered to me that it was a sign, moved me to the other side of her, and told me to be still. The Lees stopped singing and stood there staring at the rocks. They thought their song had delivered a message. The Amen Corner started praying. Mrs. Strickland shouted again, but I was ready for her this time. Our preacher got up and gave an altar call.

Everybody in the church went up and rededicated their life, except me, Grandma, the evangelist, and Cousin Wayne. I knew why I was still in my seat; Grandma told me to be still. I knew why Grandma was still in her seat; she never had to rededicate her life, hers took the first time. I knew why Cousin Wayne was still in his seat; he didn't have a life to rededicate. But I couldn't figure out why the evangelist was still sitting there. I thought he should have gone down front to help our preacher with the overload at the altar.

Grandma got up from beside me and walked over to Cousin Wayne. She took him by the hand and made him get up. She then walked over to the evangelist and told him to get up. She led them both to the altar and prayed for them a while. When they had prayed enough, Grandma brought Cousin Wayne back and had him sit by me. The evangelist got escorted straight out the back door and to his car. She told him someone from the church would send him all his records. After several hours, church finally dismissed and everybody went home talking about the sign they had seen.

As we walked on back to the house, I told Grandma, "I sure wish Uncle Sam was there."

TAKING NAMES

Our old Mill Village one-room schoolhouse closed down before I was old enough to go. I was glad because I heard my sister talk about how Mrs. Williams washed and cut all the boys' hair. She started doing that when Mr. Mudhole Cash's boys started school. She was careful not to hurt anybody's feelings, so she washed and cut everybody's hair, whether they needed it or not. The Cash boys only went to school for six days, but the tradition had begun and it lasted until the school closed.

The schoolhouse was heated by an old pot-bellied stove that stood near the back of the room. Mrs. Williams got to school early and filled it with kindling and coal. Then she took one of those colored aluminum foil-looking stars and stuck it on the floor right in front of the stove. By the time the *chilluns*, as she called them, started to arrive, the room was red hot.

She had them all hang their coats and take their seats, then she started that day's lesson. If Mrs. Williams got chilly, she had a unique way of getting herself warm. She could tell by looking down at that star just how close she was to the stove. She backed up to it and with both hands lifted her skirt tail from behind and warmed her bottom.

One day after school, my older buddy Lewis moved the star about six inches closer to the stove. The next day, when Mrs. Williams lifted up her skirt tail and stepped back on the star, both cheeks of her bottom hit the stove at about the same time. She let out a war-whoop and flat-footed Imogene King, who was sitting at the first desk in front of the stove. Mrs. Williams regained her composure, but the next day she came to school wearing glasses. She taught standing up the rest of the week.

In every class in every school in the world, there is always one self-appointed tattletale. Sylvia Sue told Mrs. Williams what Lewis had done. Lewis got a paddling and Sylvia Sue got appointed Name Taker for the rest of the year. Sylvia Sue got so caught up in the name taking, she neglected her schoolwork and failed that year. Mrs. Williams said she did not even qualify for school promotion.

When the county closed our Mill Village school, they also closed the Sargent school in the neighboring Mill Village. They built us a new brick school near Sargent and the two schools combined under one roof. The principals from both schools were given jobs at the new school. There was always a very spirited rivalry between our two schools, so the transition period took quite a while. We were now one, but we were still very far apart.

At recess, when we divided up to play ball, it always ended up being all Arnco players on one side and all Sargent players on the other. We ended up fighting just like we always had. Either a principal or a teacher had to coach the ball teams, but even they ended up fighting over how many players from each village got to be the starting players. Ball teams always have an odd number of people—baseball teams have nine positions, basketball teams have five. There was no way to have an even number of players on each team. It was a mess.

None of us had ever seen a for-real lunchroom, and the only ones that could afford to eat in there were the Mill Village supervisors' young'uns from both villages. Most of them were too sissy to fistfight, so they would take their lunchroom knives and shoot those tiny little hard green peas at one another. Problems everywhere.

When it came time to name the school, they settled it alphabetically and called it Arnco/Sargent. A major victory. But we lost when it came to school colors. We never had any, and Sargent had been green and gold for years. I can remember cussing and our girls crying when we had to dress up in school colors on festival days. It felt like I was betraying my own village.

We always had to lay our heads down on our desks and rest after lunch. The teacher could tell who had slept like they were supposed to by the size of the red spot on their forehead. The longer you slept, the bigger the red spot. Me and my buddy Bobby always cut up during rest time, but we took turns hitting one another on the forehead so we had a big red spot by the time the teacher got back from her secret room: The Teachers' Lounge. She always came back with a piece of chalk in her right hand to cover up the cigarette stains on her fingers.

Sylvia Sue may have failed third grade, but by the time I caught up with her in Mrs. Smith's class, she had mastered the art of Name Taking. She got the job again at the beginning of school after showing Mrs. Smith a printed checklist of rest time offenses that she saw in just the first two days of school. She had another sheet with all our names on it, along with a list of offenses, each with a designated number representing the offense and its severity. Mrs. Smith loved it so much she made Sylvia Sue permanent Name Taker.

Mrs. Smith announced to the class on the third day that Sylvia Sue would be watching us and taking names. Any misbehaving would be dealt with accordingly. She read the list of offenses:

1. Talking
2. Chewing gum
3. Getting out of desk
4. Throwing spitballs
5. Copying someone else's homework
6. Making faces
7. Tapping desk with pencil
8. Carving initials
9. Tampering with windows or blinds

10. Making rubber heel and sole marks on new tile floor.

The punishment you received depended on the total of the numbers by your name. The higher the number, the more severe the punishment. Punishments ranged from writing *Thou shalt not whatever-you-did-in-class*, to a note being sent home to your parents, to a full-fledged spanking.

When Mrs. Smith sent a note to Jerry's parents telling them that of the whole class, Jerry had the highest total number by his name, his parents had someone write her back to tell her how proud they were of him. They thanked her for the good teaching job she must be doing and wanted to know if he would be recognized at the upcoming school Honors Day. Jerry caused so much trouble and had so many numbers by his name, Mrs. Smith fixed some papers up in his file and helped him enroll in the Army at age eleven.

One day, I couldn't rest, but I had a headache and didn't want to be hit in the head by Bobby. I was bored and needed something to do. While Sylvia Sue went outside to dust the erasers, I whispered to Bobby and Tommy that if any of them felt an urge to pass gas, to let it go. We could have a contest to see who could do it the loudest. I couldn't see how we could be punished, as that offense was not on Sylvia Sue's list; Mrs. Smith made it clear that the list was what she was going to go by.

Bobby weighed 240 pounds in the fifth grade; he was bigger than our principal. He always wore husky plus pants with the cuffs turned up one time. Even though he was so big in the waist, the legs were always cut for a much taller man. When he turned up his cuffs that one turn, they went all the way up to his knee. If I didn't start something first, Bobby usually did. He could get away with it, most of the time.

Everybody except me and Bobby and Tommy laid down their heads to rest. They weren't expecting anything new to happen. Bobby leaned way over in his desk and tilted it up on two legs, then let out a shot of gas that sounded like one of them Whistling Chaser fireworks that Cotton brought back from South Carolina. It had a whirling, whiffling sound. It broke up the class. Sylvia Sue was still dusting erasers. Tommy went to the front of the class, turned around, bent over, and let one go that sounded like a blast from Radford Smith's '40 Ford ooga horn. Not to be outdone, I went behind Mrs. Smith's desk, sat in her chair, raised up ever-so-slightly, and dropped a serving of air biscuits.

Just as I closed my eyes to strain out the last one, Sylvia Sue walked in with her sterile erasers. The whole class got quiet. I figured they were trying to appreciate the whole effect of my masterpiece. I pushed out the last jewel and opened my eyes to watch everybody laugh. Everybody's head was down on their desk. And there, by Sylvia Sue, stood Mrs. Smith. I got up from her chair and tried to tell her I'd seen a roach bug on her desk and Grandma made me take some kerosene the night before for the croup and I was just trying to fumigate the area for her.

Mrs. Smith looked at the list. Passing gas in class was not on there. After studying it for a while, the only thing she could cite me for was getting up out of my desk, which carried a low offense number. It did not warrant any discipline to speak of. Mrs. Smith was mad at Sylvia Sue for not thinking some of us boys might try to do that. She permanently released her from the Name Taking job.

Mrs. Smith's husband was a legislator from Coweta County and she helped him write a bill that passed both the House and Senate calling for anyone spraying bugs in the state to have an exterminator license. The last I heard from Sylvia Sue, she was working for the Census Bureau.

GRANDMA
ALMIGHTY

Grandma and Mama made all my sisters' dresses. I marveled at how they turned Polar Bear Flour sacks into fine dresses with hardly anything more than onion skin patterns and sawtooth scissors. The only way you could tell their dresses from store-bought was that they didn't have a label—and they were better made.

I thought I had seen every pattern till the day I saw Mama make a sort of half-moon cut in the front of a skirt, then pull a drawstring through it. Most skirts had sashes that got me in trouble when I untied them. I had never seen a drawstring in a skirt before. The only drawstring I ever saw was in Granddaddy's old tobacco pouch.

I asked Mama who she was making that big old tobacco pouch for. She looked at Grandma and tears started rolling down her cheeks. Grandma took me by the arm and sat me down on the bed beside her. She told me that the new skirt was for my sister Mickey. This puzzled me, as Mickey wasn't big as nothing and that skirt looked too dang big for her. I asked Grandma if it was for her to be in a two-legged sack race at the upcoming school festival or something. Or if maybe the wrong size pattern had been put in the pattern box they bought from Kessler's. Grandma said, "No, it's for her to wear in a few months."

I once saw Grandma stall-feed a heifer calf in one of our chicken coops. I remember how fat that calf was when Beavers Packing Company came from Newnan to pick it up. "Y'all are gonna stall-feed Mickey and then get rid of her, ain't you?" I cried.

"I know she's tiny and frail and can't do no heavy work, but she can help me pick up bottles to earn her keep, can't she?" I noticed she'd been sick a lot lately and missed several Sundays in a row, but that was no reason to get rid of her.

Grandma calmed me down by holding me to her bosom. That clean work smell of hers had a soothing, nerve-settling effect on me. While Grandma had me in her arms, she whispered that Mickey was going to have a baby. I wondered how in the world that could be. Mickey wasn't even married. She was just in the eleventh grade. Something had to be bad wrong. Somebody was making a big mistake. I told Grandma all that and she said Mickey had slipped up, but it would be all right, with everybody's help she could make it.

I knew Mama would get the blame. Folks on the outside looking in always put the blame on somebody. They seemed to gloat over other people's misfortune and misery. Church folks were the worst at it. They got more practice because they made a habit of fault-finding and kept the gossip going.

When Mickey began to show, Grandma dressed her up extra pretty and even put some rouge on her face—but no lipstick. She took her by the arm, smiled, and walked her right in the church. On the way out, she would tell somebody how proud she was of Mickey and how she sure was glad she was going to be a grandmother. Grandma always told us to hold our heads high when adversity struck, especially if we had caused it ourselves. She reminded us that the only one we had to answer to was God Almighty and not any do-gooding Sister So-and-So or Brother Self-Righteous. She showed us in her Bible that the only thing that would keep us Baptists out of heaven was unbelief. Then she proved it by telling about some Bible characters who were real bad but got to heaven anyway after they confessed and decided to believe.

You could tell some of the good church folks wanted to say something about my sister, but they never did. They even gave her a baby shower. Mama said it was the biggest one the church ever had. Even bigger than the married ones.

I had to give them credit. They were a Grandma-fearing people.

MAN HUNT

The year I entered the sixth grade at Arnco-Sargent, we got a
new principal. Mr. Jones was a big man, combed his hair
straight back, and wore starched shirts and a tie. From the look of
him, I was sure he was an ex-evangelist. He knew a lot about
baseball and he helped coach our school team. He kept me for
hours after practice working on my pitching form and delivery; he
taught me a lot. He even got us out of playing in colored T-shirts
and blue jeans by getting the county to buy us uniforms. I asked
him one evening if Mrs. Jones got mad at him coming home so
late. He told me he never married.

I began to notice that he always walked me up to the front
porch when he took me home so he could tell Grandma and
Mama how good my pitching was coming. My Daddy had been
dead for twelve years by then and Mama still hadn't started dating.
The closest she ever got to being kissed was by Mr. Warren, and
that sure wasn't her idea.

Mr. Jones got to where he was cutting my pitching lessons
shorter and shorter and stretching his porch visits with Mama
longer and longer. Grandma would give him something to drink
and offer him a tea cake or whatever she baked that day. I knew
Mr. Jones got hot and thirsty helping me practice, but he wasn't
hanging around just for something to drink.

Mama started to fix up a little bit. On weekends, she picked all
the lint out of her hair that got stuck in it at the mill and Grandma
gave her a Lilt permanent. She started walking everywhere, trying
to get herself in better shape. I already knew Mr. Jones liked
Mama; now it seemed Mama was taking a liking to him.

Mama sat near the dugout at all my games. Every time I looked over at Mr. Jones to get a sign as to what he wanted me to do, he would be looking at Mama, trying to get a sign as to what she wanted to do. I threw the pitches I wanted and went seven and zero that year. Mama must have thrown him the pitches he wanted, 'cause he strutted around like he'd pitched a perfect game.

One summer night as we were about to start a game of chase, Mr. Jones pulled up in his light green 1957 Chevrolet Two-Ten. It was already dark so I didn't see how he could help me practice. The streetlight didn't give off much light and he could get hurt trying to catch for me. He got out of his car carrying a wrapped box, complete with store-bought ribbon and bow; his Old Spice reached me before he did. His shoes were even shined. He spoke to me and my buddies as he walked through the yard. He called me *Lonce* instead of Lawrence, sort of like Senator Herman Talmadge might say it.

When he knocked on the door, Grandma stepped outside and shook his hand. I couldn't tell what Grandma was saying, but Mr. Jones nodded his head over and over, saying, "Yes, ma'am. Yes, ma'am. I will. Oh yes, ma'am." Then he shook his head from side to side and said, "Oh no, ma'am. Oh no, Miss Bledsoe, I wouldn't think of doing that. You won't have to worry about a thing." When Grandma was through making sure he understood her Commandments, she went inside and got Mama.

The porch light glistened off the sweat on Mr. Jones' face. The only time I ever saw him this nervous was in the last game of the county tournament when we were up by one and I walked the bases loaded with no outs. He stomped out to the mound, gritted his teeth, and growled, "Come on, *Lonce*. Toughen up! Show me you got some balls!" On his way back from the mound, he was so busy looking at Mama he walked toward the wrong dugout. Ricy, our first baseman, had to go turn him around. After he got to the right dugout, I struck out the side and we won the tournament.

Mr. Jones was so nervous when Mama came to the door, he dropped the gift, picked it up, stepped inside, and handed it to Grandma. Then he turned and walked off the porch, leaving Mama just standing there. As he walked by me, I whispered to him, "Oh, come on, Mr. Jones. Toughen up! Show me you got some balls!

Grandma escorted Mama to his car and told them to have a good time. Then she took the deepest breath I ever saw her take and walked back up on the porch. She told me she heard what I said to Mr. Jones and as she went into the house, she said, "You better be the only one he shows them to."

Mama courted Mr. Jones till school started. He asked her to marry him and we all discussed it, but she decided that she wasn't ready yet. Good thing too; Mr. Jones died of a heart attack within a year. I don't think Mama could have stood being widowed twice.

Mama was about to reach the age where most people in the Mill Village realize they are locked-in to working there until their dying days. They were a proud people, but the years trapped at the mill caused most of them to take on a look of controlled desperation, like the pictures of POWs Uncle Shorty brought back from World War II. Mama started getting that look in her eyes before Mr. Jones came into her life. It was deeper now that he was gone.

I lay on the front porch swing for hours at a time trying to think of something to take that hopeless stare off Mama's face. Grandma felt an urgent need to help too, so she did what any loving mother would do. She set out to find her a man. Grandma's standards were high. It didn't take her but one Sunday morning and one Sunday night service at both the Baptist and Methodist meetings to make up her mind that there was not one man good enough for Mama in the Mill Village.

Grandma started going to Newnan every Saturday, determined to find Mama a good man—a genteel man, as she called them. That's what she always told me to be—not *try* to be, but *be*. For months, Grandma walked around the court square asking every suitable-looking man who was walking by himself two questions: Are you married? What denomination are you? It left a whole lot of men standing around with a strange look on his face.

I asked Grandma one day what would happen when she finally did find the right man. What would happen if they fell in love and wanted to get married? What would happen to her? She looked out towards the church and stared for a few minutes. I loved to watch those old, clear blue eyes stare. Without turning her head, she said that if that did happen, the man would certainly be from off the village. That Bullet, Mama, and me would probably move to wherever was close to his work. She just sat there, rolling her thumbs over and over, staring. "But why wouldn't you be going with us?" I asked. We had more than four people living in one house before. Me and her could sleep in the same room, just like always. She said that wouldn't be fair to Mama or her new man. She said she would find her a new place to live or might move in with Aunt Lutie now that Uncle Nathan had died. She hugged me real close and whispered, "I'm getting old and you're getting grown. Life has a way of changing directions now and then. We'll all adjust. Somehow."

One Sunday after church, me and Grandma were swinging on the front porch. Grandma's singing started to get drowned out by an approaching roar that sounded like a cross between Fireball Roberts' race car and a log truck. A yellow and gold 1956 Chevrolet pulled up with Mama sitting in the passenger seat. A short little man got out and walked around the car, real pigeon-toed, like Casey Stengel. He opened the door for Mama. I told Grandma he must have taken the door handles off the inside of his car. He took Mama by the arm and started across the ditch bank with her. My mouth got real dry. As Mama walked up on the front porch, Grandma stood up, but I just sat there. She grabbed me by my ear and that got me up right quick.

Mama introduced us to the fellow. His name was Mr. Marvin. I couldn't wait for Grandma to give the handshake and Commandments. Grandma stuck out her right hand and I waited for the crunch, but it never came. Just a good firm handshake, like the right hand of Christian Fellowship. I jumped off the porch and ran around back and climbed to the highest part of the black walnut tree. I sat there, shaking all over. It's him, I thought. He will be the one.

The next Friday night, me and Bullet were playing in the ditch beside the house when I saw Bullet's ears stand up. He stuck his nose in the air and started sniffing. His feet got real happy and he started running in a fit of little short circles. A low rumbling sound rolled in from the distance. It was a clear night and I had been looking over the church; I knew it wasn't thunder. The noise got louder and louder; every dog within hearing distance was barking. The lights hit the church, then turned off C Street and headed toward our house. By now the noise was deafening. It was what I feared. He was back.

I pulled Bullet low and bellied out under the hedgerow. He parked his car and went up on the front porch. Mama stepped outside and I was sure I saw her give him a hug. I looked at Bullet as if to ask *Did you see that?* Bullet nodded his head and licked my nose, clearly saying *Yes*. They went inside and Grandma stepped on the porch and called for me. One thing I learned over the years was to answer her right away. Me and Bullet started our slow walk to the house. I wondered how many more times we would get to do that.

Grandma told me to wash up, me and her would be eating supper by ourselves tonight. Mama was going out to eat with Mr. Marvin. Mama had dressed up and put powder on and fixed her hair. She put on real loud-smelling perfume and a lot of red lipstick. When Mr. Marvin passed by me on the way to his car, I could tell he was a goner. He had a goofy, glazed look in his eyes and a silly-looking smile on his face. His feet took real quick little steps and he was bending and bowing and doing all sorts of stuff that only a woman can make a man do. Me and Bullet were embarrassed for him.

Supper was real quiet, just Grandma and me. We didn't eat much. I crawled up on Grandma's big old cannonball post bed around 9:30. Grandma took my hand and we said our nighttime prayer. Even though my guardian angel was still on watch, I sensed trouble in the camp. My fortress was under attack.

The next morning at breakfast, me and Grandma didn't say much, not that we could even if we wanted to; Mama wouldn't shut up about Mr. Marvin. She was acting like he did the night before—senseless. She sang as she poured milk in my jelly glass. She dropped a pancake on my plate, then scooped it back up and giggled, asking if I was ready for another one. She flitted around the kitchen like one of Glyn Hyatt's guineas during mating season.

I asked her what we would be doing that night and she said Mr. Marvin was coming back and that they planned to go to eat at the Rio Vista in Atlanta—the all-you-can-eat catfish place I had heard about. Then he was taking her to the Fox Theater on Peachtree Street, then he promised to take her to get a hot Krispy Kreme donut at the original shop on Ponce De Leon Avenue. Whoever heard of doing so much in one night?

Later that afternoon, Mama floated off to her bedroom to start getting ready. I looked at the fake gold and marble horse clock that somebody had given Grandma and Granddaddy on their fiftieth wedding anniversary. The big hand was on the twelve and the little hand was on the two. Mr. Marvin wasn't going to be here till 5:00. That was three hours away. Three hours of getting ready? Our whole ball team didn't need three hours of getting ready for the entire ten-game county tournament. It didn't take three hours for Mr. Smith to break our garden. Grandma could kill and dress a hog in less than three hours. What would Mama do in three hours of getting ready? I was real thankful that boys could get ready—including bathing and changing underwear when needed—in less than fifteen minutes.

Me and Bullet heard the '56 Bel Air thunder around the curve at about 4:45, as it would so many Friday and Saturday nights to come. Before long, Mr. Marvin even began to show up for Sunday church services. Grandma had already done her research and found out that he was a Methodist, which according to her was almost as good as being a Baptist, but not quite.

I heard preachers say on more than one occasion that there was going to be some of all denominations in heaven, but Grandma didn't think that way. She was firm in her belief that only those of the Christian faith would get to go to heaven. I asked her about Catholics, and she said no, not a one. I was glad, 'cause that took care of Yankees; Donald said most of them were Catholic. I could not imagine spending eternity with a bunch of loud bragging about who won the Civil War.

Grandma noticed I started getting sick a lot on Friday and Saturday nights. Mama hated to go off with me deathly ill, but she knew Grandma would take good care of me till she got back home so she went on out with Mr. Marvin. After they left one Friday night, Grandma told me she knew what I was trying to do. She could see my point, but she said Mama deserved to enjoy herself after sitting at home so many years and working so hard for the rest of us. Grandma had a way of slicing your heart open and sewing it back up all in the same sentence.

One Friday evening, Mr. Marvin showed up toting an old army duffle bag. He walked in and dropped it in front of me. The solid crack as it hit the ground was unmistakable. There wasn't but one sound like it in the world. I picked up the bag and dumped it. Out tumbled five wooden baseball bats, eight American Legion baseballs—not cotton mollies like we played with in the Mill Village, but genuine leather, cork-center, nylon-stitched baseballs, all brand new—a catcher's mask, and a chest protector. He told me it was all mine. He then pulled up his britches legs to show me where he had been spiked while catching for the American Legion team in Newnan.

I ran inside and got my glove and Mr. Marvin squatted down and caught me for three imaginary batters. I struck out two and walked one, with Mr. Marvin calling the balls and strikes. I thought he missed a strike three on my last batter, but I let it go. As he got up to go inside, he pulled a brand new collar out of his pocket and strapped it on Bullet—it was the first collar old Bullet ever had. Suddenly, Mr. Marvin didn't seem so bad after all.

Mama and Mr. Marvin dated for over a year. The night he finally asked Mama to marry him, Grandma took me by the hand and walked me down to the garden. As the moon shined down on us, she told me that when a garden is first broke, it's called *new ground*. Once the crops mature, some of them stay at our house, but some are sent off the Mill Village to other places for other people. "Life is sort of like a garden," she told me, "and it's time for you and your Mama and Bullet to break new ground. But don't you worry. Someday we'll all live together again, forever."

"Sort of like all the vegetables and produce at the State Farmer's Market?" I asked.

"Well," she smiled, "sort of."

"Well I hope me and you end up in the same crate wherever we are."

WANTING OUT

Mr. Mudhole Cash and his family might just have been the best people in the whole Mill Village. Most people got jealous and resented you when you tried to do better, yet they wouldn't put forth the effort to improve their own situation. But not Mr. Cash. He and his family didn't do anything to better themselves, but other than Grandma, they were about the only ones who never talked bad about anybody or seemed envious of people trying to get off the village. He and his family would even offer to help folks move when their time finally came to leave. The whole family would smile and wave and wish them well. They may have been covered in dirt on the outside, but being genuine and down-to-earth made them clean on the inside, and that's where it counted most, Grandma said.

LaJuana, my middle sister, was determined not to end up in the mill; she studied all the time and made straight A's. When she married Buddy, she got a job at the People's Bank in Carrollton and that got her off the village. Mickey got off when she married Harold and they moved with their new little baby into a little Jim Walter home down near Franklin. Granddaddy died the year LaJuana moved out; it was the only way he was getting out. I told Mama and Grandma at supper one night that if I worked real hard when I was old enough, I might get a supervisor's job and move us over to one of those new houses the mill just built on the Carrollton Highway. At the time, that seemed like a good way out.

But then Mama and Mr. Marvin got married. It was kind of weird sitting there by my sisters and Grandma, watching my own mother get married. Even Grandma Cole, my real Daddy's mother, came to the wedding. She had known Mr. Marvin for a long time.

She whispered to me that he was a good man. I whispered back, "Yes, ma'am. But he can't call balls and strikes."

After the ceremony, Preacher Edison put Mama and Mr. Marvin down at the front of the church for everybody to shake their hands and congratulate them. I broke into a sweat as I stood there waiting in line behind Grandma. I didn't know what I was going to say to them. I tried to ease out of line, but Grandma grabbed me by the arm to make me stay. She didn't need to say a word. Her hand said all I needed to hear. As I stood there sweating, I looked at the choir loft where Mama sang her alto parts and Mr. Jackson cocked his head to reach those low-down notes, where Mrs. Fannie Maude, the preacher's wife and the choir director, wrinkled her nose and brow when somebody got way off-key—which happened on every song.

The people in front of Grandma told Mama and Mr. Marvin how proud they were for them. People always wished you the best at times like this. Just once I wanted to hear somebody say, "It ain't gonna work. You all will never be happy." Anything that might give me hope that we wouldn't have to leave the Mill Village. I couldn't believe what I was thinking. All these years I had been trying to think of some way to get us out of the village. Now, lo and behold, we finally get in the position to leave and my brain is running things around in it that I didn't understand. On one side, an angel showed me how happy Mama was. On the other, the devil wouldn't let me see anything good that might come of this.

I walked up to shake Mr. Marvin's hand and said, "I ain't going." He frowned and looked around to see who might have heard me, then rubbed the top of my head and shoved me along to Mama. I hugged Mama's neck and whispered, "I ain't going." She just smiled and kissed me and said, "Why, of course, you're not."

Grandma walked me outside and sat me down on the concrete wall alongside the church steps. Other than the marriage, it was a beautiful summer night. The moon was shining extra bright, making Grandma's face glow like she was the head angel in heaven. We were both looking up when a falling star went flying across the sky. Falling stars always sent chills up my spine. I told her I wasn't going with them. She put her arm around me and asked, "Going where? The honeymoon?"

"What's a honeymoon?" I asked. I had never heard of one. She said it was where people went after they were married, to spend time together, alone. I told her that if they didn't want to be around us, I could sleep on the back porch with Bullet. I told her Mr. Marvin was short enough to sleep on the green plastic-covered sofa. Grandma looked me square in the eyes, and said, "Lawrence, they will be sleeping together from now on."

I was shocked. My place to sleep was with Grandma, but when she went off to visit one of her other young'uns—which wasn't often—I got to sleep with Mama. Since Grandma wasn't going to get to move with us, then I would be sleeping with Mama from now on.

If what Grandma said was true, then there was no way I was going to move now. I would stay on and sleep with Grandma. I could quit school, which a lot of boys did anyway; between Grandma's Bible and her Blue Back Speller, she could teach me all I ever needed to know. I could get a job at the mill as a sweeper or doffer. Being a mill employee, we could keep the house we were in, although they might try to move us to a smaller shotgun house. We would not need a car. Between Grandma's garden and Mr. Morris's store across the road, we would always have food. Grandma cut our hair, so we wouldn't need to go to Newnan for that. Cousin Wayne just got a phone and a new TV from O.K. Vaughn's and we had a Crosley box radio that we could listen to. I had plenty of clothes and Grandma made most of hers. Besides, she could make a pair of panties last longer than Mrs. McClendon. I didn't wear shoes except to church and if my feet grew before we could afford a new pair, I'd just put them in a bowl of water to swell them up, just like Grandma did with her dried butter beans. Yep, after all those years of figuring out how to get off the Mill Village, I just about had it all figured out how to stay on.

When Mama and Mr. Marvin came back from their honeymoon, Mama said they looked at houses while they were in Decatur and found a few nice places. She said some were brick. I didn't like brick houses; I liked wooden houses. All the prettier homes on Temple Avenue in Newnan were wooden. And with wood, you could change the color every year or so. With brick, if it was red when it was mortared in place, then it would be red when it was torn down. Mr. Marvin was just trying to impress us with a brick house, but it turned me off him even more.

For the time being, Mr. Marvin moved in with us at 27 D Street and drove back and forth to his electrician job at the assembly plant in Decatur. Things were working out fine for me and Grandma—we still got to sleep together every night. Mama was happy, too. Even Bullet seemed just fine, as long as the Bel Air was parked. But Mr. Marvin soon grew tired from work and all that driving. At this rate, we weren't long for the Mill Village.

One night at supper, I told him I heard that the mill needed some hands in the finishing room. "It's a good job," I told them, "and it'll only take you three minutes to get there by car, nine minutes if I loan you my racecar—but you'll have to pull it back up the hill home—or twenty minutes if you walk, which a lot of people do." Using that flashcard math, I told him and Mama, "If it takes you four hours a day to get to and from Decatur and you work five days a week, not counting when you work the relief shift, you're spending a hundred hours a year in the car. That's more than Buck and Uncle Ezra combined. Plus, with gas at 26 cents a gallon, the way that old 327 bored and stroked engine burns gas, think how much money we'd save. We could use the extra to buy things like new baseballs. And we could use those extra hours to keep working on my pitching form." I thought my presentation went very well.

He didn't say anything. Mama stared at me with gritted teeth. Grandma never looked up from her plate. Bullet ran out from under the table. I guess he sensed Mama might try to kick me. Nobody ate much after that.

I went outside and sat on the front porch step, smelling the warm summer breeze as it passed through the old cedar tree. Bullet came and flopped down on my feet. Lightning streaked behind the clouds over the church, lighting them up like the reflection from Mr. Everett Brown's garage when he welded something at night. Grandma came and sat down beside me. "Doesn't our porch just have the best view of lightning in the whole village?" she said, tilting her face toward the sky. She kept the trees on the front ditch bank cut just so we could always have a good view when it stormed. But she always made sure to leave enough limbs in the chinaberry tree for Alvin to sit on.

As we sat there together, I wondered if the lightning would look different in Decatur. I asked Grandma if people in a big city could see the stars and moon and lightning-like we could on the Mill Village. She said, "No, Lawrence. There are too many man-made lights for them to get a good look." I started to picture life in the big city, wondering what else would be different.

"Will it be harder to get around?" I asked. Grandma said, "Yes. There are a lot of people in the city and it can get crowded at certain times of the day."

"Will it cost more?" She said yes, and told me all about tax and insurance and mentioned Uncle Sam again.

"Will the food be any good?" She said, "Have you ever seen a sign that says 'City Cooking'? No, sir. It's always, 'Down Home Country Cooking.'"

"Is it safer in the city or in the village?" She said, "The only person we ever had trouble with in the village was Cotton Smith, but he really didn't mean no harm. In a big city, people have to lock their doors and take their young'uns' wheels in after dark. And women have to be careful going out by themselves at night."

"What about schools in the city?" She said, "They're usually crowded and the teacher never comes home to visit your folks."

"And city churches?" She said, "Well, city church folks are not like our church folks. They change preachers a lot and everybody in the choir wears a robe, including the choir director. You can't get saved in a city church until the preacher and deacons talk to you to see if you and your family will fit in. They have printed up programs that they go by regardless of what the Spirit might do if it ever did decide to go in a city church. And they use store-bought communion bread instead of letting ladies in the church take turns baking it. They never have all-day sings and the special songs aren't southern gospel. They use words like *hond* instead of *hand* and *Alleluia* instead of *Hallelujah*. They sing the Doxology every Sunday. And when they have funerals, they never take the body home. They don't ever set up with the family, 'cept at certain hours set up by the funeral home." I knew Mr. McKoon wouldn't ever do that to us. He even brought folding chairs and fans to our house when Granddaddy died.

"Do people visit each other in the city?" She said, "No. People pretty much keep to themselves. And they always try to outdo their neighbors, even if they don't know 'em." I reckon it would have been cheaper on city people if everybody had Mr. Mudhole for a neighbor.

"Is there a place to swim, like the creek by Larry Hyatt's house?" She said, "They have what's called a city swimming pool and it's not open all year. You have to pay to get in and they have rules about running and diving put up on signs all around." The rules sounded like it took away all the fun of swimming.

"Do they have baseball teams in the city?" She said, "Yes, but the rich kids get most of the starting positions, no matter how good they are."

Man, I was shrinking fast. Everything that I thought I might hang some hope on was going to be left right here in the Mill Village. If it was going to cost more and everything else was going to be worse, then why in the world did we even want to leave the Mill Village? My mind was made up. I wasn't going for damn sure.

Mr. Marvin came home late one evening and told Mama that their loan was approved for the new house. That didn't sound good. Me and my buddies loaned each other stuff all the time, but we didn't have to get it approved. We just did it. I asked Grandma what it meant. She told me all about banks and borrowing and interest. It didn't make any sense. If the bank had all this money just sitting there, why would they charge us to store some of it for them? We were doing *them* a favor, not the other way around.

Mama said she and Mr. Marvin would be taking off to go to Forest Park the next day to see about closing their loan. If she took off work, the mill didn't pay her. She never took off work. This was serious. A few days later, Mama and Mr. Marvin went to Forest Park to get the house ready to move in. Mama took a whole week off for that. This was really serious.

The summer days flew by, like one of those old mushy love movies at the Alamo when they show a calendar reeling off days, one page right after another. I think I even saw a page on our McKoon calendar flip over by itself one night.

I could tell Grandma was feeling the strain of thinking she was in the way. When Mama and Mr. Marvin were home together, she tried to stay out of their way. She visited neighbors. She sometimes had Mr. Favors take her to see some of her other children off the village. They usually brought her back home after a few days. They all seemed to enjoy her visits, but they seemed to like bringing her back home the best like they all had their little family nests and didn't want her coming to roost with them.

I hurt for her. The grand old backbone of the family, mast of the family ship, our teacher, philosopher, doctor, disciplinarian, cook, spiritual guide, protector, comforter, pillar of strength was being forsaken by her own blood. I would never leave her. I would never forsake her.

About four weeks before school was to start, Mama asked me to invite all my friends over because she and Mr. Marvin were throwing me a going-away party. I told her not to bother. I would see all my friends when school started. I was not going away. Mr. Marvin came over and I knew from the expression on his face we were fixing to have one of those Father and Son talks I heard about. He told me their side of things, and how they were doing everything for me. I just looked at him and told him, "Well, if that's the case, don't do it. You and Mama leave and me and Grandma will get by. There's nothing I mind facing with Grandma."

That night, Grandma snuggled me up next to her and told me Mama and Mr. Marvin planned to move in two weeks. "I'm not leaving," I whispered. "I'm staying with you."

Grandma pulled me in close, her soft arms comforting me. She said Aunt Lutie was letting her come stay with her for a while till she was able to make other living arrangements. Everybody else's plans for the future were made, but the very person who helped get them to their future didn't have one herself.

Grandma said Aunt Lutie didn't have room for her to take all her furniture and belongings, so she would give it to her children—the very ones who would not take her in. Whatever they didn't want, she would auction off when the time came. I had seen buzzards fighting over something that was not rightfully theirs. All of a sudden I wished Grandma had been barren. I felt like Grandma was on death row and the governor had taken his phone off the hook. Her time was running out.

Grandma began to tag her belongings with names written in black crayon on pieces of wrinkled tan shipping tape. She had an idea who might want what before the rest of her belongings would be sold to the highest bidder. I watched her and I hurt every time she put a tag on something. She was being torn apart piece by piece, but she never let on.

I walked over to the old pedal sewing machine and pulled open the button drawer. The colored buttons clicked as I stirred them with my fingers. How many hours had Grandma and I spent stringing these buttons to pass the long winter nights? How many dresses and patched shirts and blue jean seats had passed over that bobbin, coming out looking new? It got Mama's name.

I looked at the big chifforobe with the drawers on the right and the full-length door mirror on the left—my second favorite hiding place for hide-and-seek. It got my aunt's name.

I sat in the chair at Grandma's dresser and replayed all those Sunday mornings I spent curled up at the foot of her bed watching her get ready for church. Right in this spot, she sat in her corset, dabbing on puffs of powder, a spot of rouge—never perfume or lipstick. She combed her beautiful snow-white hair and fixed it just right. She daubed black Griffin shoe polish first on my shoes, then hers. Grandma never spent long getting ready; nobody complains about how angels look. The dresser got the name of another aunt.

As I started to leave, I noticed Granddaddy's old foot locker and decided to take a look. Inside, there was an old Prince Albert cigar box that still had the little brass nail in the lid to keep it closed tight. Grandma had neatly stowed his pocket watch and chain, his wire-framed glasses, his old false teeth, his straight razor, and his see-through mechanical pencil that was always out of lead. The stack of letters he wrote to her while they dated sat beside the box. Every year around their wedding anniversary, she read me one of those letters. The way she read them you could tell she sure missed her man. She never cried, but I sure did. In one corner of the chest was his rolled-up galoshes and in the other corner, his felt hat down in its final resting place. She may get rid of everything else, but her man's things would be going with her. That was truly her treasure chest.

I walked into the room where the old upright piano set, all waxed and polished, and the three-legged stool where I lay on my stomach and spun round and round. At that piano, she taught me how to play I Met a Possum in the Road and part of Barbara Allen. She knew from shingling my hair that I would be able to sit still long enough to learn to play. The piano wasn't tagged yet.

The old cane bottom rocking chair where she rocked all her young'uns and my sisters and me sat by the fire. She rocked so many babies in that chair she had to recane the seat at least three times that I knew of. She was the mother of all rockers, with her big lap and slow full-cycle rock. A few mournful verses of I Saw a Wreck on the Highway and you'd be asleep before you knew it. The chair would go with her.

All her kitchen odds and ends: the polished chrome meat grinder that screwed tight to the underside of the table, the waffle iron with the black and white cloth-covered cord, the big old wooden mixing bowl shaped like a dugout canoe, the green and yellow ceramic salt and pepper shakers shaped like ears of corn, the triangle-shaped trivets she made out of cloth covered Coca-Cola caps, her cast iron skillets, cake pans, butter churn with the flowery butter mold, and her butcher knife—the one she kept sharp with a whetstone and razor strap.

When someone came to the door late at night, she answered it with a smile on her face and that butcher knife behind her back. "Kill 'em with kindness first if you can," she'd say, not knowing who might be on the other side of the door so late at night. She ran an escaped convict off our porch one night with that butcher knife. We heard a convict had escaped from the chain gang, then we all heard a commotion on the porch in the wee hours of the morning. I took my usual place behind my sisters, behind the settee, as Grandma called it. She stood her twelve gauge Ranger shotgun beside the door, hammer down—she could cock and fire faster than most men could with theirs already cocked. She wouldn't use it unless she had to. She snatched open the front door and there, trying to get in, was the convict. She raised that butcher knife over her head and charged. Cousin Wayne said he thought he heard the convict holler over the pinball machines at his beer joint. Some of the deputies saw him as he ran down the railroad tracks toward Sargent. He begged them not to take him back anywhere near that big white woman with the butcher knife back in the Mill Village. He didn't know that all he had to do was ask her for something to eat and she would have fixed him something. Then she would have talked him into giving himself up without having to use the butcher knife. *He's somebody's son*, she would think.

A few days before the sale, people began to come by and see what they might be bidding on. More hypocrites. All of them telling Grandma how sorry they were to see her have to leave and in the same breath asking her what was the cheapest price she would take for whatever they wanted. Every night, Grandma seemed to go to bed later and later. It was as if she was putting off going to sleep like she was trying to keep another day from coming.

Grandma had all her young'uns over for a supper meal. From the food she fixed, you'd have thought it was Sunday dinner. As usual, she was thinking of others and not herself. After we ate, she told them to decide who wanted what of the things she had not tagged. She went outside and sat in the swing with her arms folded in her lap. I sat down beside her and we just sat, not swinging. Every little while, we heard somebody say something like, "I gave that to her so I should get it now." Or, "This is tagged for you, but I want it." Or, "I wanted that when she died." This had to be worse than dying. Grandma's own kids were proving what she told us all along, that people seldom outright give you anything. It always comes with conditions.

The morning of the auction, these were the only words spoken at breakfast: "Thank you, Lord, for watching over us during the night. Bless all the less fortunate than us and bless the sick and shut-in. Thank You, Lord, for the food we are about to eat and for my family. Bless Nellie and Marvin and their new home. And Lord, look after Lawrence and help him grow up to be a fine, genteel man. Continue to lead, guide, and direct us and when You are done with us, I pray You will give us a home in heaven where we can praise You forevermore. Amen."

Home. Home. She asked for a home. Something she knew He would provide when her time came. Something her own children would not provide for her now. It didn't seem like a lot to ask. Not much at all. I couldn't eat.

After breakfast, Grandma dressed in her only black funeral and Sunday dress. Over it, she wore a new apron with small pockets sewn across the front to hold the money she'd make at the auction. She wore her polished Sunday shoes and finished off her outfit with a black, wide-brimmed Sunday hat. Where the fake rose had been, she tucked a fresh red rose from her garden.

The auction was to begin at 9:00. At 8:00, she walked to the church and went inside to pray. When she came walking back up the hill half an hour later, Mr. Mudhole and his family were with her. She gave Mr. Mudhole some tape and a crayon and told him and Mrs. Cash to go mark whatever they wanted and it would not cost them a dime. And if he had trouble spelling his name, to just put a big X on the tape and she would make sure it would not be sold.

Unconditional love.

As the trucks began to pull up out front and the people began to arrive from all over the village, I climbed up on the banister at the end of the porch. A cloud was making up over the church. Thunder rolled in the distance way back off toward Newnan. Grandma walked out on the porch and folded her white-gloved hands across her stomach. She told all the people how much she appreciated them coming and that she made tea cakes and fresh lemonade for all that would partake.

As she stood there talking, a ray of sunshine sliced through the dark clouds and poured straight down on Grandma. When she stepped closer to Mr. Dutton, the auctioneer, the ray of sun seemed to follow her. She took a deep breath and looked up at the sky like she was looking for the corner of heaven where she knew her mansion was being prepared. I realized she knew that the altar had been made ready and she upon her faith had taken her place.

She squeezed my hand and whispered, "I love you." As the auctioneer's gavel fell, I wept openly and prayed for God to spare my Isaac.

The Goat Man

Arnco mill village ballfield
dugout

Arnco mill village ballfield from
behind home plate

Arnco mill village ballfield from
pitcher's mound

27 D Street

J Rob and Nellie Cole

Arnco Mill Village Church

Grandma Bledsoe

CPSIA information can be obtained
at www.ICGtesting.com
Printed in the USA
LVHW050514041120
670657LV00004B/279

9 781953 300171